Advance praise fo

Share or Die

Herein lies the real lesson of the Internet. It may not be the
one that marketers and investors want to hear, but it's the
key to understanding the way people and businesses will
be interacting in the peer-to-peer, digital reality. It's also at
the heart of the current renaissance – an overturning of the
scarcity-based, highly centralized systems that have been in
place since the 1300's, and a rebirth of the values that make
human society work.

—Douglas Rushkoff, author, *Program or Be Programmed*

If you're a well-meaning, well-educated, generous person,
and you can feel yourself being cornered and hammered
relentlessly by a faceless, wicked, out-of-control economy,
then *Share or Die* is the book for you.

— Bruce Sterling, blogger, author and journalist

I wish I'd read this book when I graduated. I wouldn't have
been less lost, but the beautiful voices, stories and experiences in these pages would have helped me understand that,
before I could find myself, I had to lose myself first. If you
know someone who dreams of something bigger than being
part of the rat race, please give them this book.

—Raj Patel, author of *The Value of Nothing*

Smart, funny, irreverent, resourceful, committed, vision-ary – these terms come to mind as you read the passionate voices of the first net-native generation. *Share or Die* not only depicts and explains the daunting challenges facing young people today, it delivers some very good news: A monsoon of creative, positive energies is already shaping a better future.

—David Bollier, scholar and activist of the commons, blogger at Bollier.org, and Cofounder of the Commons Strategies Group

A new system is being born and this book is an important record of it. This is nothing else than a book of active proph-ecy for our times.

—Michel Bauwens, founder of The Foundation for P2P Alternatives.

SHARE
or DIE

SHARE or DIE

VOICES OF THE GET LOST GENERATION IN THE AGE OF CRISIS

Edited by MALCOLM HARRIS with NEAL GORENFLO

new society
PUBLISHERS

Cover design by Diane McIntosh.
Illustration © iStock (penfold)

Printed in Canada. First printing April 2012.

Paperback ISBN: 978-0-86571-710-7
eISBN: 978-1-55092-503-6

Inquiries regarding requests to reprint all or part of *Share or Die*
should be addressed to New Society Publishers at the address below.

To order directly from the publishers, please call toll-free (North America)
1-800-567-6772, or order online at www.newsociety.com

Any other inquiries can be directed by mail to:

New Society Publishers
P.O. Box 189, Gabriola Island, BC V0R 1X0, Canada
(250) 247-9737

New Society Publishers' mission is to publish books that contribute in fun-
damental ways to building an ecologically sustainable and just society, and
to do so with the least possible impact on the environment, in a manner that
models this vision. We are committed to doing this not just through education, but through action. The interior pages of our bound books are printed
on Forest Stewardship Council®-registered acid-free paper that is **100%
post-consumer recycled** (100% old growth forest-free), processed chlorine
free, and printed with vegetable-based, low-VOC inks, with covers produced
using FSC®-registered stock. New Society also works to reduce its carbon
footprint, and purchases carbon offsets based on an annual audit to ensure
a carbon neutral footprint. For further information, or to browse our full list
of books and purchase securely, visit our website at: **www.newsociety.com**

LIBRARY AND ARCHIVES CANADA CATALOGUING IN PUBLICATION

Share or die : voices of the get lost generation in the age of
crisis / edited by Malcolm Harris with Neal Gorenflo.

ISBN 978-0-86571-710-7

1. Cooperation. 2. Cooperativeness — Moral and ethical aspects.
3. Sharing. 4. Generation Y — Economic conditions. 5. Generation Y —
Conduct of life. I. Harris, Malcolm II. Gorenflo, Neal III. Title.

HD3271.S52 2012   334   C2012-901348-X

CONTENTS

WORK

Preface
NEAL GORENFLO

About six months ago, a weather-beaten, middle-aged man asked me for money on the platform of the Mountain View Caltrain station.

I gave him three dollars. He thanked me and asked what I did for work. I introduced myself and learned his name (Jeff), and we shook hands. I pulled a card from my computer bag and handed it to him as I told him that I publish an online magazine about sharing.

Jeff lit up, "Oh, I get that. When you're homeless, it's share or die."

That got my attention, and I asked him to explain. Jeff said that a year earlier, his girlfriend had drunk herself to death alone in a motel room. He said she wouldn't have died had someone been with her. For him, isolation meant death.

Jeff explained his perspective further: He has no problem giving his last dollar or cigarette to a friend; it comes back when you need it. But there are those who just take. You stay away from them.

I asked him about the homeless people in Mountain View, which is in the middle of prosperous Silicon Valley. Jeff said there are 800 homeless people in the city and that each has a similar story.

That conversation got under my skin. I shared it with Malcolm Harris the next day during a call about this book. Half-joking, I suggested Jeff's phrase, "share or die," as a title. At the time, I thought it was over the top. I wasn't serious. But Malcolm began using it in correspondence about the book. It stuck.

My conversation with Jeff marked a turning point in my thinking. I had thought of sharing as merely smart because it creates positive social, environmental and economic change through one strategy.

But Jeff's story and the directness of his phrase—share or die—broke through my intellectualization of sharing. Jeff helped me see something that I was blind to, even though I knew all the facts—that sharing is not just a smart strategy; it's necessary for our survival as a species. This has always been so, but today our condition is especially acute—we're using 50 percent more natural resources per year than the earth can replace. And global population and per-capita consumption are growing. It's now glaringly obvious to me that we need to learn to share on a global scale—fast—or die.

But the threat is not only one of biological death. Those like me, who are in no danger of starving, face a spiritual death when we act as if well-being is a private affair, and gate ourselves off from the rest of humanity with money and property. We can neither survive nor live well unless we share. It's my outrageous hope that the young voices in this book will do for a generation what Jeff did for me—wake them to the idea that sharing can save them and the world.

Foreword
CORY DOCTOROW

This was supposed to be the disconnected generation. Raised on video games and networked communications, kept indoors by their parents' fear of predators and the erosion of public transit and public spaces, these were the kids who were supposed to be socially isolated, preferring the company of video-game sprites to their peers, preferring Facebook updates to real-life conversations.

The Internet's reputation for isolation is undeserved and one-dimensional. If the net makes it possible to choose to interact through an electronic remove from "the real world," it *also* affords the possibility of inhabiting the "real world" even when you've been shut away from it by your fearful parents or the tyranny of suburban geography.

Even as entertainment moguls were self-servingly declaring "Content is king," they failed to notice that content without an audience was about as interesting as a tree that falls in the deserted woods. Conversation is king, not content. If we gather around forums to talk about TV shows or movies or games or bands, it's because we enjoy talking with each other, because "social" is the best content there is. Content is just something to talk about. That's why the telecom industry—the industry that charges you to connect with other breathing humans—is 100 times larger than the entertainment industry.

Which is to say that our "disconnected" generation is more connected than any generation in history—connected via a huge, technologically augmented peripheral nervous system of communications technologies that gives them continuous, low-level insight into their peers and the world they inhabit. Which is not to say that being wired up to the net's social radar is an unadulterated good: adding capacity and velocity to your nervous system can be a recipe for disaster, creating race conditions in which minor disagreements snowball into vicious fights, where the bad as well as the good can find itself magnified through positive feedback loops that ratchet minor stimuli into feedback screams. There's a downside to everything.

But let's look at the upside for a moment. Let's look at what connectedness means for people whose economic fortunes are in decline, a generation facing joblessness and a crashing dollar, a contracting economy and the austerity virus, which lays waste to our common institutions from libraries to subways, schools to community centers.

For that generation, connectedness is a way to coordinate, to work together to achieve goals, to substitute electronic connective tissue for wealth in the great race to *get stuff done*. Nearly a century after Nobel laureate Ronald Coase's seminal paper "The Theory of the Firm," it's clearer than ever that the better your organizational system, the more you can achieve. Market economies reward well-organized firms with wealth, but in Coase's world, money is mostly a way of scoring who gets the most done with the fewest meetings, memos and other forms of institutional overhead.

As the one percent hoover up the world's fiat wealth, we're all faced with finding non-market ways of getting stuff done—housing ourselves, feeding ourselves, educating and entertaining ourselves. And that's where connectedness shines: the cheaper it is to get all your friends pulling in the same direction, the more you can get done for less money—whether that's founding a housing co-op or occupying the financial center of your city.

Share or Die isn't just a book about generosity or compassion; it's not just a repudiation of greed. The thread that runs through all these essays is the way that connectedness makes it *feasible* to share—feasible to seek out your ideological peers and collaborators, feasible to share the product of your collaboration with the world, feasible to turn your experience into a set of instructions for the next group to follow, refine and republish.

There's a lot of anger and disillusionment in this book, and there's some blind optimism and more than a little naïveté. But more than anything, this is a book of realistic hopefulness, a book that showcases creative, thoughtful people who are learning that there are alternative paths to happiness, that wealth is more than money, and that connectedness is at the core of community, no matter whether it comes through a virtual world, a social network or a face-to-face interaction.

Introduction
The Get Lost Generation
MALCOLM HARRIS

A sk a headline writer at any paper of record and they'll tell you that today's young people are "the lost generation." They tend to use this label as if Hemingway and Fitzgerald hadn't stumbled their way through half the bars in Paris under the same flag. Unfortunately, the youth of today aren't lost in a morass of sex, art, booze and politics (not necessarily in that order), but rather can't find a path through the haze of economic insecurity and impending ecological catastrophe. The current use of the term draws less from those charmed ex-pats than from "the lost decade," the name given to Japan's period of economic stagnation during the '90s. But the two uses point toward different aspects of sociohistorical lostness: one is about a generation not knowing what to do with its capacity within society, the other about a society that doesn't know what to do with its capacity for generation, a world that seems to have already made too much of everything. It is unclear in which way my generation is lost, whether it refers to the seemingly misdirected lives of 20-somethings or our potential that may go unrealized due to the employment crisis and overproduction—unless we open new paths. Having read the essays that follow, I think it's a bit of both.

Of course, the absent jobs that could make us "productive" members of society go a long way toward answering the question of direction. Young people are semi-autonomous when it comes to our life choices, but we are subject as a population to economic and environmental conditions; one could say we are lost because we have been lost. Even so, we don't seem to be going anywhere. The new phase of "emerging adulthood" described in the now infamous *The New York Times Magazine* article "What Is It About 20-Somethings?"[1] involves a return to the parents' home (as in Lauren Westerfield's "Flexible Lives, Flexible Relationships"). Nothing could be more "found." There is also some irony in calling the most connected generation in the history of mankind "lost." The phone in my pocket can tell me not only where I am but where I might want to go next and how to get there. There are ways in which we could not get lost if we tried.

Or could we? If the directions through which productive potential is traditionally realized (traditional careers, families, housing, modes of transportation) are not going to be open to many of us, as the situation indicates they will not, then we will need to produce and construct new ones. "Make it new" is an old phrase but, from one generation to another, it's still good advice. The original lost generation produced its enduring works of art in flophouses and dive bars, not offices or writing workshops. For the modernists, being lost was a precondition for creation, not a barrier. We have no choice but to cease to think of exploration as a bounded time in which we are to "find" ourselves before we are put to work. For many of us, that end may never come. If the roads are closed, getting lost becomes the only way to move. The alternative is stagnation and the bare-life instrumentality of the on-demand labor contract. (See Ryan Gleason's "The Janus-Faced Craigslist.") We have better things to do with our productive capacities than depress wages for those who cling to traditional employment. Instead, we have the opportunity to create new forms of social organization and patterns of mutual support.

Instead of "finding ourselves," I think my generation would be better off losing ourselves. The selves we can hope to find ready-made and waiting are not what we've been promised, what we've prepared for (see Sarah Idzik's "Unprepared") or what we want. If the traditional job market fails to accommodate so many young people, then the modes of living devised by and for our parents will remain impossible for us. I mean this not only in terms of living lives centered around consumption and but also in regard to the physical habitats they've built. We will live closer to one another as we realize distance is not the same as safety. In order to survive and even have a chance to live, we will have to build communities of cooperation rather than competition. Learning to live together instead of merely in proximity to each other will be crucial. (See Annamarie Pluhar's "Screening for Gold.") Sometimes getting lost will require us to leave some small possibility of prosperity behind and jump into the unknown. (See Emi Gennis's "Quitter" and Jenna Brager's "Who Needs An Ivory Tower?") Sometimes it means leaving any sort of normal stability behind and taking only what you can carry (Nine gives her inventory in "Take It And Leave It") in search of something truly desirable.

The obvious but tricky question is, Where can we go that is away from this dominant relationship, away from the selling of our lives and planet chunk by chunk, so as not to die? Both the alienated suburbs of my childhood and the costly cities of my adolescent dreams seem unlikely sites. There are places where capital and the state move too slowly, corners they cannot assimilate: the warehouse shells of an exhausted industrialism, the foreclosed homes that hold the ghosts of a dreamed America that never came to be. During Milicent Johnson's adventures in Detroit, she found a city inventing with what's there, moving past what's gone and into something different. There remains space and time where horizontal networks can survive and grow, where new practices can spring from the scrapheap generated by late capitalism.

Young people can organize themselves under new forms, such as cooperatives (see both of Mira Luna's essays on co-ops) and nomadic communities (see Robin's "Every Guest A Host.") We can depend on each other's living labor rather than the dead value stored in commodities. A shared future means less stuff, which means less digging for more fuel to burn. Networks of collaborative consumption allow people to share goods in common without the burdens and costs of personal ownership, which means less time buying and more time living. If families are those groups of people against whom we refuse to fight in the race up the ladder, then young people are going to get bigger families. Do-it-yourself becomes the best option (as in Melissa Welter's "Eating Rich, Living Poor") and, luckily, ever more feasible as the means of production become more accessible to individual producer/consumers. We must be suspicious of everything we do not build, of everything handed down from an empire in decline, and look to our own hands.

Even while the lives we build are independent, they're still shared, and sharing is what we're gonna need if we're going to get out of youth alive.

WORK

Things as Which I've Been Asked to Dress
Life in the Nonprofit Industrial Complex

SAMANTHA MILLER

illustrations by **ADRIENNE CANZOLINO**

'm an organizer, but when I tell people that, they either think I'm a party hack or I rearrange people's closets. "Activist" is in most people's vocabularies, so professional activist is an easy way to explain that on and off for the past six years my job has been to build a movement to the end the wars in Iraq and Afghanistan. I've organized protests, marches, sit-ins in Congress, dance riots in the streets, giant public art projects, speaking tours and student activist trainings. I've chained myself to an oil barrel, built a blockade out of school desks in an intersection in downtown DC and danced in a war profiteer's lobby with a few hundred other kids. Sometimes I was being paid, sometimes I wasn't. This is my work, and most of the time it's my job.

I always had an instinct that capitalism was a dirty word and that my destiny did not involve working for a corporation. All those downtown office buildings and people in suits completely motivated by profit seemed repulsive to me from a young age. Until I turned 20, I had only vague notions of activism and radical politics. I figured my choices after college would be to get some random office job for a corporation or small business, manage a doctor's office like the two generations of women in my family before me, or become a lawyer or teacher. (I had ruled out anything involving too much math and science a long time ago.) I didn't know what nonprofits were, and definitely did not know I could cause trouble for a living. Then I found a women's anti-war organization with an office down the street from my college apartment, and the world of professional activism quickly opened my eyes.

To work for an activist nonprofit, you have to be just idealistic enough to work way more than you're being paid for but not so idealistic that you're not willing to constantly compromise for funders, the media or because your boss wants to go to the President's fundraising dinner. Adaptability is also necessary—an activist's job shifts and changes along with the political landscape. You might organize a protest one day, meet with a congressperson the next and be running a Facebook petition campaign the next week. It also helps if you're attractive, able to blend into a variety of settings, don't mind making a complete fool of yourself and are just generally willing to do things your mother likely told you were rude or unacceptable in civil society.

"Nonprofit" is a big, statutory umbrella that includes churches, arts organizations, corporate foundations, schools, unions, advocacy organizations and a variety of other tax shelters. If advocacy organizations were a big happy family, activist nonprofits would be that crazy aunt you feel a sad but abiding affection for but also secretly hope gets too stoned to remember to show up for holiday dinner. Advocacy nonprofits actively try to create social change. They do this in varying degrees of scale and effectiveness, using a large array of strategies and tactics. They also spend a great deal of energy scrutinizing their own and other's scale, effectiveness, strategy and tactics, which often results in lengthy articles, blogs and Internet flame wars between people in these organizations who disagree with each other. Even when myopic, politics is never boring.

Advocacy nonprofits and activist nonprofits part ways at

the border of "the system." Advocacy nonprofits work inside the system; activist nonprofits try to work both inside and outside of the system. Activist nonprofits essentially put a brand and a tax ID number on social movements. For those of us who want to create radical change, such as overthrowing capitalism and the state and creating autonomous communities based on mutual aid, this has a whole ton of horrible implications, all of which are well documented. (For more on this, check out the excellent collection *The Revolution Will Not Be Funded*, by INCITE: Women of Color Against Violence.) This story is about survival and compromise, the things I do sometimes for a paycheck, sometimes because I believe in them and sometimes for a combination of the two.

Most professional activists, including me, have organizing projects that we do in our free time as well, often a more radical version of the work we do at our jobs. This is what keeps me and my industry friends sane. The work I want to do and the work I get paid to do sometimes intersect, but if there's a costume involved, it's pretty safe to say that that action is solidly in the "paid" category.

The following is a partial list of the costumes I've worn as part of my jobs or internships.

The Spirit of Justice

A statue in the Department of Justice building in DC depicted the Spirit of Justice as a woman with one exposed breast, which John Ashcroft had covered when he became the attorney general under President Bush. The costume involved a pink peace-sign nipple pasty. This was within the first month of my first internship.

Wolf in sheep's clothing

This one required wearing an awful headdress (involving a sheepskin head-band and wolf ears) outside a very expensive fundraiser in Beverly Hills.

Media whore

I wore a French maid lingerie thing along with fishnets, black spike heels and the logos of major news corporations all over the exposed parts of my body.

I Miss America

For this I dressed like Miss America in a pink sequined gown but with horrible messaging that implied there was a time when America was super-great.

Pink policewoman

I don't have an excuse for this; it's just wrong under any circumstance.

Member of a pink religious choir

This was also in the halls of Congress.

Pregnant woman

I was trying to sneak helium balloons into a congressional hearing. Let's just say capitol police were not too happy about me walking in looking nine months pregnant and leaving with a reasonably flat stomach.

Cow

Actually, I was the lead cow in a small herd of cows in Congress harassing some jackass senator after he made an extra-special comment about social security, tits and milk cows.

Sometimes I get sad when I think about these costumes and all the ridiculous, downright counter-revolutionary shit I've done working for these organizations. I hate the police; why would I wear a pink police uniform? I pushed a bed in front of the capitol and got a bunch of people to roll around in fake money while listening to Ol' Dirty Bastard—it had something to do with government being in bed with the oil companies. Then I think about what most of my DC anarchist friends were doing and (not that I'm judging) I am

Things as Which I've Been Asked to Dress : **11**

thankful that I've never done canvassing, dog walking, medical research studies or Craigslist sex work.

Sometimes I decide that at least establishment activism is better than being totally complicit, but then I get sad again. Radicals go to the root of problems, and the root cause of every issue I've worked on is capitalism. Nonprofits don't go there. Sometimes they talk about "corporations," but no one will name the problem, and no one will even go near trying to address it. Nonprofits deal in reform because you can't deliver revolutions in time for foundation funding cycles.

The organizations that make up the anti-war movement are an especially sad breed because they have no sense of strategy. They operate on the notion that if there are enough protests and media stories, politicians will feel pressured to end the wars. Successful activist nonprofits, like many in the environmental movement, identify achievable goals, target power-holders and develop strategies to win better conditions for people's lives. After eight years of war in Iraq and almost ten in Afghanistan, the anti-war movement has just recently started to think about strategies and campaigns to actually end the wars.

I once found myself at an event where then-Senator Hillary Clinton was speaking to a room of college feminists on Capitol Hill, hosted by the National Organization of Women (NOW). I was working for a women's peace organization at the time and knew that my boss would be hosting a fundraiser for NOW at her house in LA later that week. I was also familiar with Senator Clinton's voting record; she was one of the most conservative Senate Democrats, who frequently voted in favor of the war in Iraq and parental consent for abortion (both of which NOW was opposed to, at least according to their website). The number of contradictions in the room was already enough to make my head explode, and then Clinton proceeded to give a speech about all the wonderful things the US was doing for the women of Afghanistan. At that point, in this miserable moment, the stars aligned: I turned on my video camera and stood in a doorway leading to a small foyer to the right of the stage, having convinced a security person I was one of NOW's interns. As Clinton ended her speech to a flurry of applause, she was led off stage with a small gaggle of women through the very doorway where I was standing.

I was suddenly in a small room with Hillary Clinton, the president of NOW, a few other important ladies in pantsuits—and no security. No one had noticed me, and I was still filming in the corner of the room. I couldn't just stand there and do nothing; that would go completely against what I had been taught in my previous two years as an activist. So as they were posing for pictures, I saw my opportunity. I loudly blurted out something about how they should all be ashamed of themselves because Hillary Clinton is a warmonger and is doing nothing for the women of Iraq except voting to keep bombing their homes. Not my most eloquent moment, but it got their attention.

Clinton quickly exited the room as the president of NOW and a very indignant woman with a lot of blond hair confronted me. We had a heated exchange in which I berated the women for supporting Clinton and her policies, and said they should be ashamed to call themselves feminists. They told me I should be ashamed of myself, which is when I thought it was a good idea to start dropping my boss's name. The incident ended shortly thereafter, and I went back to my office to regroup, call my boss before someone else did and watch the footage. My boss was semi-horrified but not totally upset, and I didn't get fired.

A few days later, Hillary Clinton announced her candidacy for president. NOW quickly endorsed her; my boss held a lovely fundraiser for NOW, which included a polite critique of Clinton's policies; and a few of us started scheming about running a spoof presidential campaign for Condolleeza Rice.

During the Bush years, liberals were throwing money around left and right to support activist organizing. It was relatively easy to get jobs or short-term contract gigs organizing random protests, street theaters and arrestable actions—especially if you were in DC. The best job I ever had was organizing a day of coordinated direct actions in DC on the fifth anniversary of the US invasion of Iraq. This was the only time I was paid to do work I completely believed in—I spent three months organizing logistics, outreach, resources and action plans, coordinating with about 20 different organizations to pull off a dozen distinct actions in downtown DC. We were modeling horizontal organizing structures, solidarity across tactical divides and a creative vision of what protests can look like beyond a boring rally and permitted march. Politically, we were offering a holistic analysis of the pillars that uphold the military-industrial complex, military recruiters, taxes, oil companies and other war-profiteering corporations, lobbyists, Congress, the media and the security state.

But that was early 2008, a few months before the Democratic and Republican national conventions and subsequent protests that summer. The national conventions in 2008 were the last hurrah of a fading national anti-war movement. With the onset of Obama-mania and the recession, the national coalitions fell apart and regrouped under weaker banners. The organizations with the largest bases suffered rapid attrition and lost funding. Three years later we're still trying to figure out what happened and how to fix it.

Ever since Obama's presidential campaign, progressives and left-leaning folks are even more divided, many of them still making excuses for the president and the Democrats and refusing to oppose them in any way. These days, I find myself spending much more time behind a computer than in the streets. Like most of my peers, I've found employment in communications and social media. Now I run websites and databases instead of organizing actions. When there's no funding for organizing, everyone still needs a website, and can trick their funders into believing that online activism is a reasonable replacement for physical work. Instead of sit-ins in Congress, I create "online actions" where people can click a few buttons and e-mail their Representatives. I hated wearing a pink police uniform, but I hate exclusively online activism even more. However ridiculous we were, being face-to-face with Karl Rove and trying to arrest him has to be better than bombarding his office with e-mails. Facebook and Twitter do not make revolutions; they are tools. They mean nothing without the people using them, and no matter how many friends or followers an organization has, the nonprofit communications professionals of this country are not going to create an American Tahrir Square.

All this being said, I still think professional activism is a lot better than any of the alternatives I've tried. Capitalism is an awful, oppressive, broken system we are forced to exist in, and until I decide to completely drop out and start an anarchist collective permaculture farm off the grid somewhere, I have to work. Now I work with veterans and military families trying to end the wars. I make a living wage plus benefits, and I choose my own hours. I generally believe in the work I'm doing, and even when I don't, at least I never have to do anything I think is completely awful. It may not be the revolution, but it'll do until we make that happen.

Unprepared
From Elite College to the Job Market
SARAH IDZIK
illustrations by EMI GENNIS[2]

've lived in Chicago, first as a student then as a working resident, for six and a half years now. But I didn't vote in the pivotal mayoral race held here recently.

I still list my parents' address in Pennsylvania as my "permanent address" on anything requiring one. I don't have health insurance through my employer, a travel company in downtown Chicago, because I'm still on my Pennsylvania plan, even though I've worked here for nearly three years. I don't have a dentist here. Or an ophthalmologist. I've never even been to the new primary care physician I selected through my insurance. And I still hold a Pennsylvania driver's license.

Why is this? The answer is fairly simple: I still don't consider myself a full-fledged resident of Chicago. But the reason for that is a bit more complicated.

In high school, I was smart. Really smart. I knocked out A's like I was baking cupcakes. Teachers loved that they could count on me. But I was small-town, public-school smart, the kind of girl genius who plows through her secondary education without too much resistance. Deep down, despite my excellent grades and my involvement in a bunch of extracurricular activities, I knew that I hadn't been challenged enough to be as cocky as I was. When it came to college, I had two options: I could play it safe, stay close to home and go to school in Pittsburgh, where I would benefit from the "big fish in a small pond" effect. Or I could take a leap and accept my offer of admission from the University of Chicago.

The prospect thrilled and terrified me. Everything the school promised sounded utopian: the academic rigor, the immersive intellectual energy, the dense core curriculum filled with great books that sparked constant meaningful discussion. But the school also prominently promised, on all of their prospecting materials, to challenge me. They said they would force me to defend myself and the positions I took, force me to think deeply, to see all the angles. I knew I'd been handled with kid gloves so far and that Chicago would be an insane leap outside of my comfort zone. Not to mention the shock of being so far away from home (what was this alleged "Midwest?") in a place where I knew virtually no one.

But in the end, I decided: nothing ventured, nothing gained. I flopped like an enthusiastic mudfish out of the small pond and into the lake.

Now, like anything, university had its ups and downs. Not every class is inspiring; not every teacher is interesting; and, of course, not every assignment will take precedence over a new and interesting social life. But ultimately, it would be nearly impossible to count the ways in which I benefited from my education (much, in the end, thanks to that social life). I was, as I suspected I would be, somewhat behind from the start, and the learning curve was steep. Most of the time during those first two years it felt like just about everyone I met was a genius. My friends were brilliant. My classmates were all well read and eloquent. I was so green and, I thought, underprepared. I had an embarrassing moment during a movie night with my new dorm-mates when I revealed I didn't know what NATO was. Despite what a guidance counselor might have thought from my high school transcript, I didn't have the aptitude for the university's rigorous academic and intellectual life; I had to learn it. But in the constant presence of people as smart as or smarter than I, under their influence in class, at dinner, hanging out in someone's dorm room—everywhere I was in contact with other people—I learned quickly. It was like taking up a foreign language through immersion.

Eventually, I got more comfortable with the rhythm of things. I learned to ask questions, to read carefully, to be inquisitive, to poke around in all the dark corners of a text or a thought and to follow the strands of thought wherever they may lead. I felt like I was aging in dog years, absorbing more, learning and maturing more quickly than I could have imagined possible for myself. But that kernel of insufficiency planted in me in the beginning still never goes away. It changes shape, maybe, becomes something slightly different, but it instilled in me a driving force, my raison d'etre: to be better and to learn more. Constantly and forever. My life's quest became and has remained the struggle for self-improvement through knowledge.

Learning, true learning, is like cracking open the door to a universe: once you've experienced it, everything else spreads on and on right before your eyes. The more you learn, the more you find to learn. You can never know enough. I had found what people go to college to find: direction.

Unfortunately for me and my fellow classmates, the culture of learning is not necessarily compatible with the culture of the market. I was an English major, and not one who was diligent in seeking internships while in school. My expertise was literary analysis. What I considered to be probably my highest achievement was my exploration of Milorad Pavić's postmodern hypertextual novel *Dictionary of the Khazars*, for which I found myself researching and downloading examples of the obscure genre of hypertext fiction (way bigger in the '90s) and writing about the subjectivity of names and definitions, the existential crisis of reading a book without its own narrative velocity, and the futility of the self-guided attempt to achieve simultaneity of all the information in the text. Who wouldn't want an employee who could do that?

Of course, the thing I hadn't yet faced was that my literary skill would not directly translate to a job. The ideals I had internalized and learned to dedicate myself to made me the kind of University of Chicago student they let rave in the brochure, but they weren't the same skills I would need to survive in the real world.

"The real world" as an expression is apt. For all of my feverish intellectualism, I was in a charmed environment. Perhaps it was a necessary part of my education, but college functioned as a protection, a safe haven, a free pass of sorts, and it did not reflect the reality of life outside of it. For me and my classmates, the transition was destined to be particularly difficult. We had less warning than past generations did; we had so much less time and energy to spend focusing on the future. The kind of education I got, priceless though it was, is tricky to spin into a proper post-college career even in the best of economic times if you don't have a sense for where you're going once you step outside. I did not have that sense. Most of my friends, largely students of the humanities and/or theater, didn't either.

Inevitably, the clock ran out on us all. Graduation rolled around and dumped us on the other side, where we were within grace periods for our student loans but not for long. A life philosophy of inquiry and a fairly elite diploma didn't protect us from the immediate exigencies of rent, jobs and stress.

I knew I was at a disadvantage, not having the career-boosting professional degrees that some of my more technically minded peers had. Like my friends, I had a world-class education and ambitions to be great, but only the vaguest of ideas about what I even wanted to do.

Some people, though no one I was close with, were fortunate enough to have parents who were able and willing to foot the bills for a grace period of post-college finding oneself. The rest of us had to do it on the fly, scrambling for work in what we knew was a quickly deteriorating economy, while trying to work out what sort of path we wanted for ourselves. The word "job" was precious enough; the word "career" seemed outlandish, absurd, almost unseemly. My ambitions had shrunk alongside my options; we went from expecting greatness to expecting respectable work and then to hoping for something that paid.

I was naive about the real world much in the same way that I had been naive about academic life. I searched for jobs primarily on Craigslist. I didn't know what to do with my résumé. I had enough money from my graduation gifts to last only a couple of months unemployed in Chicago; after that, it would be back to suburban Pennsylvania. Browsing job postings, I realized I had no idea what I was even looking for. Jobs were scarce, let alone appealing gigs. Furthermore, I was totally unqualified, based on the advertised requirements, for anything but clerical administrative work. All that I had learned, all that I had overcome and accomplished—and here I was scanning dozens upon dozens of ads looking for the rare few with the words "administrative assistant" in them.

Not knowing what else to do, not having any clue or any direction, feeling the hot breath of unemployment breathing down my neck, I applied to all of them.

I managed to get lucky—and despite my degree, it does feel like luck. I had a job by July, the result of one of the applications for which I had, by this point tired and getting lazy, attached my résumé to an e-mail and just dashed off a paragraph in the body about how great and bright I was. This is the same job I have now, almost three years later—a gig at a small travel company typing and printing travel documents for unbelievably wealthy, entitled globetrotters who won't read any of them. This was about as far from the highbrow literature of my undergraduate years as construc-

tion work. I was terrified to start an actual nine-to-five job; it seemed like a myth, something surreal, something that couldn't touch my life.

After starting, the disbelief soon gave way to misery. The day-to-day experience left me feeling utterly crushed. I wasn't creating anything, I wasn't really doing anything of any consequence at all. I got on the bus every morning, exhausted, with all the other people who worked in offices downtown. I walked into the office every day, sat at the same desk, in the same chair, did the same things. I adopted the same bubbly, pleasant attitude as my coworkers, with whom I felt no connection at all. It made no sense to see them as real people I might connect with since, after all, I felt like this was not where I belonged: an office in an industry that had nothing to do with my life, a job in which I had no real interest. I had nothing invested in my job or my employer. I did what I had to do: hammer out the work, play nice. But I felt all day long that I was inhabiting a strange bubble, separate from where I really lived my life, removed from anything that affected me or that I cared about.

But the bubble expanded to fill such a large part of my days that I started to despair. During office lunches, when I sat at the conference table eating pizza while my coworkers talked about the best time during the week to pick up ornamental plants at Home Depot, I sometimes felt so detached that I saw myself hovering above the table, watching the me sitting below. I was an alien who had just woken up in a strange place with a broken compass. Several nights in the first few months I came home, took off my coat, sat on the couch and starting sobbing inexplicably and inconsolably. I had crying jags in the bathroom at work. I was falling into a dark hopelessness. I hadn't read a book or written anything new since before graduation. I finally started to appreciate why TV is so popular: when you're working a day job, who has the energy or will to do anything more at the end of the day than collapse on the couch with a bag of chips and an NCIS rerun? I gained 15 pounds in 6 months.

And still, I did not leave my job.

It sounds like stupid or self-destructive behavior. I was suffering. I was miserable. For my own good, I should have left long before now.

But I stayed because I was too terrified to leave. The economic situation was bleak and not improving. All I had to do was look around at my friends, the best and the brightest, to see it. One woke every day at four o'clock for the morning shift at Starbucks, trying to get enough hours every week to make the minimum for health insurance. One interned in local government, but afterward was forced to take up his old job at the zoo. One had to move back with his parents in Iowa. Several waited tables. Two toiled miserably in low-level jobs at law firms. Out of everyone I knew, there was only one real success story—only one person who had secured a job in the appropriate field that set her on the career path she wanted. Further schooling was an option for the shell shocked or potentially so; my boyfriend took refuge in another year. One friend defected to grad school in Austin, Texas. Everyone seemed to be in the midst of the application phase at any given time, working on getting into grad school for something or other, anywhere but here, anywhere but the real world, where there was little work, and even less fulfilling work.

My job was almost insultingly low-paying, and I was living paycheck to paycheck, as we all were, cutting it too close to quit with no other offers. When I got home, I trolled the Web for hope of better opportunities, but jobs were so few that I found just about nothing, certainly nothing that I would want to do more than what I was already doing. I was interested in the arts, but with the economy tanking and arts

funding even more constricted than in normal lean times, a paying job was a far-off dream, and I couldn't afford to do an unpaid, or even low-paid, internship.

It was jarring. Not just for me, for all of us. It seemed to make so little sense. The banal necessities of the actual struggle for survival in the world were at odds with our sense of the world as some kind of meritocracy brimming with possibilities for genuine intellectual growth, a place whose purpose is to provide those opportunities. Having the unquenchable need for knowledge that we all had worked hard to develop, we had also acquired a unique capability for dissatisfaction—something most of our parents had never had the luxury to experience, especially so acutely and so early in life.

This dissatisfaction is a luxury, but also a curse. My peers and I, perhaps sometimes even despite ourselves, believe in the higher purposes we learned in class, the value—sacred-ness, even—of knowledge, inquiry, curiosity, justice, the pursuit of truth. If we can be said to have a collective moral compass, that's it. My friends and I trust in the values that our liberal arts education set out and succeeded to instill in us. But sitting in an office typing away meaninglessly? How were we supposed to understand that as part of the world we had imagined, or had been taught to imagine?

This disconnect made me think I might be going insane. As though my head had been metaphorically severed from my body. The realization that I had little beyond my job to fill my days and justify my existence terrified me. Was this who I was now? A stranger to myself, typing away inconsequentially in an office somewhere in the West Loop, with no bright shining future?

I felt stranded, lost, paralyzed. And I resisted dropping anchor in a place so toxic. My attitude toward my work was distanced; it was impossible to develop any feelings of loyalty or any desire to chase upward mobility or permanence when I couldn't stand the thought of actually caring about such a dull job. I remained unsettled, like a nomad pitching a tent on fallow ground, refusing to get too comfortable. It was bad enough that I was totally rudderless, that I had no clear professional aims or goals to speak of, but add to that what had become our culture's collective recession-fueled terror—I couldn't say how many times I heard the warning, "At least you have a job"—and you have a bona fide total inability to climb out of my rut.

Unable to keep the nine-to-five levees in tact, my work situation had metastasized into a very miserable work/life situation. The expansive, freeing sense that I had once felt, seemingly lifetimes ago, that my life's possibilities were endless had shrunk down to the size of a pinhead. The area of possible movement seemed to be so very small, not just for me, but for all of us. We still wanted great things, but they seemed so impossibly distant, so indulgent, when the basic fact of work wasn't even a given.

Everything we wanted, everything we really valued, was

offset by the reality of "normal," traditional work. We had no idea how to navigate this world, but our education didn't fail us—it instilled in us a dissatisfaction for this kind of life.

I didn't have the confidence to go searching for personal success. I had had the momentum, the take-the-bull-by-the-horns wind, sucked right out of my sails. For almost three years the kernel of dissatisfaction has grown inside me while I've allowed the things I truly valued to be subsumed by the empty immediacy of survival. I doubt we will see the full effects on this generation for decades to come, when we'll start to understand just how far-reaching is the tentativeness that has developed within us these last few years.

But now I'm preparing to take another leap, just like I did when I went away to college. I'm going to try to marry the ideals I am so loyal to with the very same life necessities that generated my stagnancy and depression. I want to integrate the spirit of inquiry and the pursuit of knowledge

into the way I make my living and create my own version of the real world—a lesson I never learned in school, and for which I have absolutely no blueprint. Again, I enter a new situation underprepared but optimistic that my capacity for dissatisfaction will actually serve me well this time as a trustworthy guide.

I'm planning to leave Chicago this summer to start over. I'll move somewhere where I can finally put my feet on the ground: grow roots, get a new driver's license, get a new permanent address. I want to make friends and build a community with interests deeper than the potted plants at Home Depot. The goal is to stop feeling like such a listless wanderer in the story of my own life. Maybe I'll even find a new dentist.

Quitter
EMI GENNIS

SHARE or DIE

Take It And Leave It
Inside the Pack
of a Modern Nomad
NINE

This pack was a departure present from colleagues at my first office job, which I left to go traveling in Canada when I was 18. I'm 33 now, and this pack been around the world and back since then. It has been emptied by American, Australian and Kurdish officials, left out in the rain by Norwegian baggage handlers, soaked through with sweat in Macau, and used as a seat anywhere I've been left waiting. When it finally developed a tear recently, I was going to replace it but realized it would be cheaper and more sensible to have it mended. Plus, it felt wrong to just discard my pack after so many

years of loyal service. The tailor in London said it was a fairly arduous process, but the pack looked good as new and, at £20, was far cheaper than a replacement.

Netbook

I'm a freelance writer and editor, with emphasis on the editing if you're talking about jobs that pay. I'm qualified by pedantry rather than by my degree—sociology with gender studies was never something I expected to get me far, though I did spend several years as a staff member at a support project for sex workers. I opted for self-employment when funding was cut two years ago and I was laid off. Since then, my netbook is about the only significant thing I've had to buy, making it possible for me to work while traveling. It's small enough to fit into my shoulder bag without anyone guessing there could be a computer in there. It has introduced me to aspects of the 21st century I was slow to adopt, such as Skype and Wifi, which I still kind of interpret as magic air. It has a USB mouse that a stranger from the Internet gave me in Edinburgh when his office was getting rid of some stuff. My business is called "Out Of This Boring Neighbourhood," which is a line from a song by the anarcho-folk-punk band Defiance, Ohio, but the name takes on additional meaning every time I gather my things and move.

Ancient mobile phone

People laugh at me because it's so old and can't do anything fancy, but I don't really care for hi-tech gadgets. I already use the Internet too much; I don't need to be switched on even more. When I'm overseas, I don't bother buying local SIM cards. It's mostly there so I can tell the time, be contacted by friends and reach help in an emergency. I send text messages only if I really have to; otherwise, I call and hang up, leaving friends "missed call" icons on their phones to signal agreement with a plan or to let them know I got home safe.

Money

I raided my childhood coin collection for currency from countries I expected to visit in the near future, which I have merged with money from places I've just left. I've got Euros, pounds sterling, American and Australian dollars, Swedish kronor, Iraqi dinar, Turkish lire, Malaysian rringgit and a coin from pre-handover Hong Kong, which I figure I can maybe still get away with. Last year I had a bank account that didn't charge for foreign transactions, but those days are over. Now I need to withdraw large amounts of cash in one go to make the charges worth it.

Sometimes I don't get any work for a month or more, but I have enough of a safety net, plus I'm enough of a cheapskate, that I can cope without it for a while if I really have to. Because of these fluctuations, I don't keep to a strict budget but play a fun game called "What Is The Absolute Least Amount Of Money I Can Spend Today Without Having An Utterly Miserable Existence?" Greater financial stability would be nice, but a regular job would mean I couldn't keep moving so much. I weighed up the pros and cons and this is the result.

Books

I stopped buying new books after I joined the redundancy club. At the moment, I'm traveling with one book I won in a blog competition, one book I bought cheap in a second-hand bookshop, one book I was given years ago and one book lent to me by a friend. At least a couple of these will be passed on to others when I'm done with them.

I write this from Leipzig, where I'm cat-sitting for a month. Having a postal address here means I can look forward to receiving another book in the mail; before I headed out into the world, I selected titles that I was willing to part with, listed them on BookMooch.com and sent them to people who requested them. Now when I hear of a good book, I add it to my BookMooch wish list, which seems to get me over the psychological hurdle of wanting it instantly; eventually, if someone lists their copy, I'll get a notification e-mail and I can use some of the credits I've accumulated.

Clothes

Most of my T-shirts were purchased new, but I'm no longer adding to that collection. Any clothes I acquire nowadays are hand-me-downs or the odd charity shop discovery. My stripy sweater and corduroy trousers came from a friend in Chicago last autumn. My waterproof jacket was £5 in the Leigh-on-Sea PDSA (People's Dispensary for Sick Animals) shop. My green V-neck sweater came from a free shop in Edinburgh, my khaki trousers and cloth bag from a friend in Barcelona who was clearing out his possessions in advance of a move to Copenhagen. I don't care much for shopping anyway, and these clothes hold memories of the people and places they came from.

Footwear

I bought my Kung Fu slippers in Barcelona for €5 when I was reconsidering my options after heartbreak caused me to leave Berlin in a hurry. Whenever I have a base camp for a while, I wear these around the house. When I'm in hot countries, I wear them out and about.

I bought my trainers for about £45 a few years ago, back when I had stable employment. At the moment they're still covered in mud from Iraq. They get leaky and I've thought about replacing them, but if they don't get a chance to dry after it's been raining, two pairs of socks will get me through.

Passport

It's obnoxious that an EU passport affords me so many privileges, but I'm not going to argue. I find cheap ways of getting around the world thanks to airport listings on Wikipedia and the painstaking notes I make as I scroll through them: Istanbul to Colombo, Colombo to Kuala Lumpur, Kuala Lumpur to Gold Coast—that's Turkey to Australia for £280, and two extra countries along the way, a few days in each. In Australia I'll visit friends and look after somebody's dog for a few weeks. After that? I don't know. Maybe New Zealand. When I became self-employed, I figured I couldn't leave Europe again until I had a stable income. It hadn't occurred to me yet that I could justify it if I didn't have rent to pay.

Guiding principle

When I figured out where I didn't want to be, but didn't know where I did want to be, I decided to remain open to any opportunities that came my way. This means that at times I don't know where I'll be in two weeks or a month, but if I hold on long enough, something will turn up. The basic setup is this: I seek out cheap routes and accept detours; I visit friends, couch-surf with strangers, and enjoy space to myself by taking care of people's homes and pets while they're on holiday. After a while, you get used to the short-term nature of everything.

Keys

Eventually, some day, I'll return to my flat in Edinburgh. Till then, my best friend is living in it, paying most of the mortgage, and forwarding mail once in a while, when I have

Credit: Nine

an address to give her. I have no idea how long I'll keep on traveling. I just know I'm not ready to go back.

Once in a while, I feel really kind of lost. Sometimes I'm sad for no good reason, but that would also happen were I to stay home. I remember when I had more security, be it work, a routine, a partner or some kind of stable social space. But I also remember that there were reasons behind my decision to leave. Before I left Edinburgh, I was bored and frustrated, drinking too much and behaving badly, and I think it's better to see the world and go home only when I can be certain I won't return to more of the same. Meantime, I'm happy most of the time with what I'm doing and where I am, and I appreciate the connections I get to forge along the way.

There isn't much of a script for what I'm doing. I'm not one of those people who saves up, quits their office job and travels around the world in the appropriate order for exactly one year. I'm not a smug freelancer whose office is a beach hut in Thailand. And I'm not daring enough to hitch across a continent by myself and camp by the side of the road.

And still, others tell me that they could never live the way I'm living, that they're not brave enough. But I don't think it takes much, really. You need to be resourceful and confident, reasonably streetwise but also open to the prospect that most people are basically good. The kindness of the people I meet on the road continues to overwhelm me, and I aim to both repay it and pass it on as far as possible.

I feel like I'm cheating slightly, with my passport and financial reserves, and I want to stress that those financial reserves are finite. But two facts remain: one, I'm still in a better position than many, so I'm not going to moan about how broke I supposedly am, and two, these are strange times and nothing is guaranteed any more—if it ever was. So I make the best of what I've got. I fell into what I'm doing now thanks to the choices that were taken away from me, and with them went the reason to stay home.

Heartbeats and Hashtags
Youth in Service
HANNAH DRENCHER

You're a what?" He screams into my ear, combating the bass of the speaker propped between us.

"A vol-un-teer," I repeat, this time louder.

"So, you like . . . make no money?"

"Nope, no salary for an entire year!" The guitar cuts off midway through my sentence and I am left screaming in the middle of the bar.

This is the point in every one of my "a volunteer walks into a bar" stories at which little blue antennae suddenly sprout up through my curls and the person across from me seemingly forgets how to form coherent sentences.

Yes, I know we are in a recession. Yes, I get that a $25 weekly stipend is hardly enough to buy a Metrocard, never mind spend a night out in New York City. No, you don't have to worry about me affording this drink. Yes, I actually chose to do this for a year.

I am answering every one of his questions in my head. He doesn't actually ask them, but I can tell they are practically bullying his tongue, begging to pop out of his mouth. Instead, he keeps them tucked in his cheek and asks a single question instead, enveloping them all into one neat pile: "Why would you ever do a thing like that?"

It is a good question, but encounters like this keep me fumbling for a good answer to pair with it.

Society has already forcibly stamped "Generation Y" on my forehead, at the sight of which older generations stop and scour the floor in search of my pacifier. My generation is (supposedly) the innovative but impatient, the smart but selfish. So, in an attempt to avoid talking about the massive "Y" on my face, I find it easier to talk about my second indelible mark: "volunteer."

I am 22 years old, dedicating my first year out of college to a service program in the Bronx, New York. And though it is not always easy to keep it simple in New York City, I am getting quite creative when it comes to making 25 dollars stretch across an entire week or even quite diligent at keeping the whole stipend intact until the weekend so as not to be the charity case in a sequined skirt come Friday night.

Though my major living expenses are covered, the recession isn't exactly taking it easy on me. I still get daily wake-up calls from the $60,000 of college debt that has taken up permanent residence at my heels. I am still knee-deep in the slush of a muddy economy right beside my peers, feeling the cold shun of a job market that has shown itself to be quite stingy with the young and hopeful.

When people hear "volunteer," they picture a girl with empty pockets and a full heart resting her head on newly fluffed pillows of Hope and Change every night. I won't argue against the full heart, and while I do make wishes for world peace from time to time, I usually just find room to hope that my peers and I will emerge from this recession having learned something valuable, having taken it as a chance to be innovative, motivated and out-of-the-box with what we can offer to the world, whether the job market has its arms wide open for us or (more likely) not.

"Can you get us into that book everyone is talking about?" She looks up at me with hope that I might understand.

"The book?"

"Yes, that book on the computer." She wipes a child's nose, reaching between the peeling plastic cereal box lids on the food cart. "You are good with computers, right?"

"Do you mean Facebook?" I ask.

"Yes! That's the one! Everyone keeps saying we need that."

Two weeks into my volunteer year, I found myself itching for more opportunities to serve in the surrounding neighborhood.

While my three other roommates work in the Bronx, teaching English to immigrants and coordinating daily activities for homeless women and their children, my volunteer work takes place in a non-governmental organization's office on 43rd Street. On a daily basis, my work there is far removed from the borough that I longed to get to know beyond the week or two I spent on alternative spring break trips in college.

The urge to get more familiar with the borough led me just one street away from my apartment in the Bronx to Sister Margaret and her community life center, a place I could easily give spare hours to when my work in Manhattan wasn't demanding a solid eight hours from my day.

Sister Margaret is the executive director of a community life center that doubles as a nervous system connecting people throughout the Fordham neighborhood. I met her in person after, for the first time since I was 12, a Google search failed me and produced no results, no number to call, no e-mail to contact. The search engine spat back a blog that had not been updated since 2008 but was meant to suffice for a center that serves over 2,000 people daily with everything from immigration services to housing.

We spoke for a while about the time I could give her and the roles I could play. She offered me a spot as an assistant teacher. I would spend my time guiding children to the bathroom and pumping hand sanitizer into a pinwheel of little hands.

"I can sing songs. I can dance. I can color. I can do whatever you need of me," I told her. "But," I continued, swallowing hard, "do you need some help with your website?"

And that was the moment, the very first moment since arriving in the Bronx, that I no longer felt like a helpless volunteer who would leave in 12 months without having made an impact. For once I was not burying myself in a pile of social problems with no foreseeable answers, or sulking over the fact that it would take me the whole year to unearth just the questions I had about poverty in the Bronx. I had begun quilting my own purpose: to build a new website for her life center, to get her "into that book," to lace together the strings of social media with the cords of social good.

If my generation knows one thing extremely well, it is social media. We know the utility of Facebook and how to put up a Wordpress site in ten minutes flat. We get the impact of Twitter and we can tag like we were back in elementary school and the streetlights hadn't gone on yet. We were raised with our fingers click clacking on several surfaces at the same time, and although the adult media depicts us as motivated self-starters swinging around some serious entitlement issues in this bad economy, I tend to believe we are getting pretty good at this whole "pushing forward" motion, turning our résumés from white flags into paper airplanes.

"What do you want people to know when they look at the website?" I ask her between doodling notes and potential color schemes onto a fresh pad of yellow paper. "Beyond a theme or layout, what do you want them to see?"

We are cramped into a tiny office space she has made for me, officially embarking on a branding and identity process for her life center, but I've already noticed how this small, cluttered desk and old computer greet me much better than my desk in Manhattan. The space she has made is welcoming and warm; the wood surface in replenished daily with pictures, brochures and documents from throughout the years to help me understand the history of Sister Margaret's labor in the Bronx.

"That we don't help people here," she says, running her fingers over the front cover of an annual review created ten years ago, before picking it up to thumb through the pages. "I want them to know that we help people to help themselves. We may give them the services, but they do the rest."

She goes on to tell me how the center began 30 years ago with a single cup of soup and a roll, how helping one individual through a soup kitchen led to six organizations sprawling and giving throughout the Bronx.

Even with all the relentless cuts in social services, Sister Margaret still keeps her vision for the center in pristine condition as if she opened her doors just yesterday with chicken noodle soup and a roll in hand.

"I'd like to see us open up a nursery in the future. That's one of my dreams, to be able to extend childcare for newborns." I am scribbling her words furiously onto the yellow pad, my fingers aching to jot down every dream she digs up before me, every plan she still has for the center even in an aching economy.

Throughout the weeks of collaboration and planning, plotting a whole new look and an interactive site, I learned that Sister Margaret is an expert on beating hearts. She understands the slow, symphonic beat of a woman who has just lost her job and cannot afford to pay her rent or feed her children. She tunes into the quick, strident beats of a stampede of four-year-olds as they pour out into the playground after nap time. And the awe of it all is how she manages to translate every single beat, fast or slow, into a social service for someone in need. The woman is a master when it comes to matching heartbeats with social services, but she knows nothing of online social networking. This is where the recession is hitting the life center the hardest. Sister Margaret struggles with money, grants and cuts in funding, all while trying to keep up in a world that updates its status every five minutes. She deals with hundreds of flesh-and-blood individuals every day, but falls victim to a society that thinks she needs a better website.

But in the name of service and what I now know to be compassion, the two of us, spanning a 40-year gap, take time every day to teach one another. She teaches me to stay fixated on heartbeats even in an economy that hypnotizes with dollars signs. I teach her the sounds of social media cooing in the ear, the Zen beauty of a minimalist setup on a website, the pulsating potential of a blank Tumblr page. Together we show one another what is inside the box and teach how to use it to work outside. We work to close a generational and economic gap with heartbeats and hash tags, every single day.

"Can you change this job description for me?" She hands me the piece of computer paper. "Tell them that I want you. Everything that you did, I want that again."

She needs to update the job description of the position I have held in the past six months and send it back to my supervisors for next year's volunteer. I've done nothing listed in the first description and so I draft a new one, packed to the brim with my own added hope that the next volunteer will be competent enough with keyboard shortcuts to keep the online networking of this life center afloat.

SHARE or DIE

A knot forms in my stomach as I think about leaving this place, of another someone coming into my spot and learning to tie up whatever I leave undone, but I think of all the progress that has emerged from this one year, a year that I thought would just be a waiting period. I thought I would wait out the storm of the recession, stalling until the job market chose to embrace me and my generation. But that wasn't the way it worked out.

The Janus-Faced Craigslist
Comedy, Tragedy and Video Games
RYAN GLEASON

This is a story for the young and aimless. Well, scratch that; this is a story for certain people who consider themselves young and aimless. This is for the young Americans itching in the wake of college or for the ingenues who threw themselves into a new city, desperate to paint or sing or scribble their way out of anonymity. If this story is going to work on any level, you have to know a bit about me. Don't worry, there really isn't much to know. I can spell myself out as such: a 20-something (the lower half), degree-holding former English major, gratingly liberal, open-minded and excited—or just naive. That's what this story is about: me, the sap, and the class mobility that let me jump from highbrow humanities to lowbrow (physically speaking) scrubbing of toilets with a few stops in between.

About two years ago, after managing to earn a humanities degree from a public university, a feat that requires some attendance, some manual bullshitting and some heart, I decided I'd move from the DC area to Seattle. Sure, there were reasons. I had a friend out here (something I've since learned we in fact all have); we had cowritten a comic book, and we were going to make it all happen. I dragged along some fellow grads and off we went, road-trip style. The road trip was uneventful: beautiful landscapes, subsequent pictures, drinking, smoking and the occasional hijinks. We made it to Seattle—go figure. Days ticked off like seconds and before we knew it, my friends and I had a place to stay, complete with rooms and mattresses of our own. This is when the economic pressures made themselves abundantly clear.

First, the credit card. I had busted most of that on the way over. My early swipes of invincibility with the card marked my road trip attitude, but like any good vanishing point, by the time I had to settle down and act like I lived in Seattle, my financial outlook was nonexistent. And second, the unemployment. It's not like I expected that by becoming a comic writer I would just stumble upon stacks of money eagerly waiting for me under my new doormat. You know, I just thought, well, I thought I wouldn't plop myself down and say, "Now what?" The comic was a trickle, we needed a new, unpaid illustrator, needed to shop it around, needed to care, and I needed some money; but really I guess I was just dazed, crammed into a corner of the nation I knew nothing about. Where was my scholastic spine? My reassuring professors? My indispensable skills of interpretation? I needed to shut the fuck up and get a job.

So we needed the Internet. The Web's call became an ever-present drone among my roommates and me. We were headless job hunters if we didn't have our netz, more specifically, our Craigslist. Oh, Craigslist, where would I be without your endless stream of hand-me-downs or your vast stacks of scams, gigs and jobs? I have turned the Craigslist free section into material mounds and then into kingdoms. Are its seedy networks ushering in an era of digital agoras? I won't say, but I can attest that my bare Seattle home was transformed by Craigslist for the mere cost of the gas and the sweat it took to haul people's unwanted stuff. If I hadn't directly benefited from all this free nonsense, I might be concerned. I mean it's a perpetual loop of shedding things (they really do become mere things)—pictures you upload to an ad, just screaming neglect, begging to be whisked away by another owner. I don't like the attitude, but it has blessed me with plenty, which was just what my friends and I needed to jumpstart our life-building efforts. Furniture of ▪▪▪▪▪ ▪▪▪▪▪ ▪▪▪ ▪▪▪, ping pong tables, bad art, televisions, blenders, organs (musical or otherwise) and—most-most-*most* importantly—most of the jobs I've ever landed.

But for a while we didn't get the Internet installed at our new place. The details behind this are fuzzy. I think it was a mixture of laziness, indecision and maybe some identity verification. Whatever the reason, we were hitting up the public access—a lot. This is very trying for any young fuck who just assumes a browser is built into his arm. Unsurprisingly, cyber cafés (a term as outdated as "modem") were scarce. We went to the libraries and waited our turns to "surf" (cue ancient poster of kids marveling over a screen glowing digital green). A member of Seattle Public Library is entitled to 75 minutes of access every day The clock starts as soon as you sign in. For the jobless this means a manic rush to update résumés, scan Craigslist (or as we've affectionately dubbed it: "the crag"), prepare letters, get 'em out, rinse, repeat. If you can't reflexively alt-tab between pages, you are dead in the water. We would each average 20 to 30 applications a session. From there you just have to wait. Landing an interview in the seas of the crag is tricky. There are things you can do to game it, little tweaks I refuse to go into, but at the end of the day it's a crapshoot. Is an employer going to open your e-mail among hundreds of applications? Are they really going to like what they see? Whatever, keep applying. This went on for about three weeks. And then Nintendo called me. Well, sort of.

It wasn't Nintendo; it was a contractor they were using to edit games, and they wanted me to review grammar.

Compared to the no job that I had, this seemed like an easy call. Nintendo! I like(d) video games! They made Smash Bros! I wanted to be a bro! Of course I'll take the interview! I'll gulp system-clearing potions to weasel past your drug tests! I'll sign a piece of paper that says I get nothing but my meager money and that I understand that one day, possibly very soon, you will simply call to inform me I no longer work for you. I will not even think the words "union," "401K" or "dental." I'll do it all, and more, with a smile.

None of this is really shocking, Craigslist job pages are plagued by an overpowering number of ads for limited-engagement, project-oriented work. You'll usually find said ads saddled right beside listings by temp agencies clamoring for your attention and assuring you of the brilliance of your many qualifications. Agree, and like part of a demented collection, your name will become yet another row in their massive archive of the area's technically employable. This all speaks to the mindfuck that is searching for jobs in such a gaping crag. Being an at-will employee means that your relationship with the company can be ended by either side at any time—no liability, no hard feelings, no severance pay. No union, no worker protections, no vacation time. In all likelihood, if you're a recent college grad, you've never felt so disposable. But for a video game company that needs to put in a quota of hours of review before their products hit international shelves, this sort of contracted work is standard operating procedure. Logic and destitution were licking the spindly hairs on the back of my neck, so I took the job. No further deliberation? Nah, I just wrote off the toil and doubt; a paid job meant my life in the city could continue.

What did I do exactly? I fixed in-game grammar. Translators turned the original Japanese into choppy English and I fixed the holes. If this sounds like fun, then I'm writing it wrong. I'd work on one project at a time, for weeks and weeks until my thumbs ached and eyeballs burned. There wasn't much accountability. I had to a) not fall asleep and b) move my hands, press controller buttons and keep my eyes on the screen. Aside from all that, I could be utterly empty. I was just a numerical contribution to a mandatory inspection, the reassuring (English-fluent) human presence that Nintendo needs to make everything check out. That reality, at times, was oppressively dull. Video games often have endings or just well-worn tracks, and once they run their course, you can move on. That is, unless you're getting paid to do just the opposite. Going through the same motions Monday through Friday allegedly looking for subtle in-game flaws simply stunned me; dismissing the "if you fall asleep, you're fired" risk was no longer an option.

Most of my coworkers didn't have a problem. Detailing them won't do me any good, but let's just say there are plenty of folk who can never turn off when it comes to video games. When they had breaks, these folks would bust out portable systems or video game magazines or their patented fanboy babble. I remembered what it felt like when I left my gaming machine on for too long and it got red hot, a sure signal that it was time to pick myself up and do something, anything that didn't require a TV screen; well that's what these people feel like all the time, like a red-hot box of fried wires, burned-in pixels. I should also mention some of the awful diets I witnessed, including a horrifying breakfast combo of chips and Mountain Dew, a sight that is sadly becoming more and more common. Nintendo wants you stay healthy (isn't that why they built the Wii?), but they are also more than fine with indulging contracted workers with strategically situated vending machines.

Even if it wasn't back-breaking labor (more on that soon), it was frustrating to see my creative dreams mashed into controller grime as I cycled through text screen after text screen. I was depressed over my contribution to the entertainment industry, often wondering how society had arrived at the point where customers found joy in what was, for me, drudgery. Are kids so restless that being bombarded with a constant stream of novel games really is the pinnacle of fun? Probably, but I didn't have the energy to address the issues that were keeping me employed. I was resigned to keeping on working until they pulled the rug out from under me.

Why didn't I just leave? I could have kept applying, interviewing, etc. until something better stuck. I could attribute it to the outrageous attendance expectations of contracted workers or I could say it was the soul-fucking length of my commute (Seattle to Redmond is nothing, unless you jam it with every car, everywhere, all at 5 p.m.). The reality probably has more to do with my contract and my lack of money. The contract has a fatalistic draw to it; I think I wanted to see how long I would hold up before they axed me. There was something painfully fun about the idea of being hurled to the curb by Nintendo, told to fend for myself. The scramble to see what's next for the old sap. Interestingly enough, plenty of the contractors I knew loved Nintendo so much that they would get canned, get in line for unemployment, and then wait until Nintendo's contractors offered them another gig. This cycle gave them ample time to simulate their former jobs within the comfort of their very own parents' homes.

I lasted four months before they cast me aside. My historic inability to save while working a wage job continued, my last paycheck going straight to my credit card and rent. Based on my ATM statement, I had about ten days to find something new, so I renewed my Craigslist frenzy, resolved to take whatever came first. The winner was house cleaning, and let me assure you that house cleaning remained the winner as it proceeded to whip my ass. I had worked my share of physical jobs, had done the restaurant thing and wasn't keen to do it again; so I thought house cleaning would be a great break. I quickly learned I am terrible at cleaning anyone's house, let alone the houses of people whose standards and wages are high enough for them to regularly pay cleaners. My childhood chores meant nothing. I left streaks on everything, couldn't get the hair off of toilets, and missed dust and spots constantly. When I discovered the existence of my lower back through a surge of toppling pain as I vacuumed yet another stairwell, I knew I was officially broken. If I hadn't quit when I did, they surely would have fired me a few days later.

That's pretty much the story. Plenty of new work happened after that, and despite all the credit evaporating out of my card, I didn't have to crawl back to the parents. Of course, it wasn't all that bad all the time. My work week was a drag, but I was living somewhere brand new. Seattle life was swirling all around me; it was my respite, my justification. They have lots and lots of water here, big trees, smatterings of culture everywhere! And on a regular weekend, I would get hammered and commiserate with the similarly precarious. When it really comes down to it, my life has always been a far cry from any sort of real misery. There are padded buffers all over this place. I came with the education; I came with the Internet, the credit card, the car that got us here. Many people simply can't say the same. I am one of the fortunate ones, this experience being my first foray into making it in whatever urban job climate you want to call Seattle.

Take away what you will, be it the reality that more and more people are going to get contract work with numbing conditions, no benefits and no guarantees, that Craigslist is some sort of virtual thrift store deity or that cleaning people—not me, I mean the ones who have been at it for years— deserve immense respect. But understand that survival in whatever environment you choose means unpredictability. One day you're playing video games for a living, the next you're back at the library. You won't always have to spin the at-will employment wheel and take whatever new gig comes your way, but these days when jobs are tough to find but easy to lose and careers aren't hiring, sometimes you have to sit down on your Craigslist couch and figure out what's next.

Emergent by Design

VENESSA MIEMIS

t's October 2010, and I'm reclined in an all-expenses-paid seat in business class on a flight to Berlin. I'm going there for two weeks to collaborate on a video project with a couple of artists I met online, then flying to Amsterdam to present the video to a room full of bankers at the largest financial services conference on the planet. I'm not a media producer; nor do I work in the financial industry. All I can think to myself is "How the hell did I get here?"

Rewind about a year and a half, and I've just started an MA in media studies at the New School in NYC. I have a vague sense that the Web is the future, and I want to understand what that means. I make the commitment to do the program full time for two years. My husband thinks this might be my way of avoiding "getting a real job" for a while.

The thing is, I had a high-paying corporate job. Counting salary, benefits and the free car, it was paying me well over six figures. Though the job was rather soul-deadening, I had no idea what the alternative would be, and I was scared to lose the sense of security it afforded me. I figured I'd just keep doing it until I had a nervous breakdown or they fired me—whichever came first.

Turns out it was the breakdown, but not the way I'd imagined.

I got a call from my father one afternoon telling me my mother, a vision of health at the age of 49, was in the hospital because of some stomach pain. Hours later she was diagnosed with stage four terminal ovarian cancer. It was completely out of the blue, and we were shocked. For her own reasons, she chose not to do the surgery or heavy chemo and instead tried to rely on natural and alternative therapies. She fought bravely but ultimately passed away shortly after her 50th birthday.

This was a pivotal moment for me, and at 25 years old I was asking myself, "What the fuck am I doing with my life?" I realized how quickly everything can change, and I refused to waste any more time doing a job that left me empty. Why bother being unhappy when I could be dead tomorrow?

So I quit.

I was determined to find a calling that brought meaning and purpose to my life, and I spent time trying various things. Finally, after being involved with a Web start-up and feeling invigorated by the pace of change and innovation in that field, I made the decision to go to grad school.

Though I didn't have a vision of where my studies would take me, I was constantly inspired by how social media were being used to effect positive change in the world. So I started a blog (EmergentByDesign.com[3]) of observations of what was going on. I got on Twitter too—not to amass followers, but to discover information faster and from curated sources.

Without my really paying attention to what was happening, my blog started gathering more and more readers, and my network on Twitter continued to grow. My strategy was pretty simple: respond to each comment left on the blog in a respectful, well-thought-out manner. Reply to every tweet and retweet. Invite generative dialogue.

By doing this, I started building actual relationships and trust with people, even if it was only in 140-character bursts or short comment replies. I found that the Web can be an effective medium for building community by being honest, expressing authenticity and vulnerability, and leading by example when it comes to the kind of interaction and engagement one expects to receive. Curiosity and playfulness help too.

The more ideas and explorations I put out there in my posts, the more they attracted like-minded individuals from around the world to respond, give me feedback on my thoughts and offer amazingly helpful links and resources I would not have found otherwise. People wanted to help me and seemed vested in my success and eager to share in my victories. What an amazing feeling.

As energy and momentum gathered, it seemed like people were waiting for us to do something together. But I didn't know what to suggest. The idea of open distributed collaboration and cocreation sounded great, but how did you go about it?

The first project that manifested itself was Junto, an idea for an open discussion platform. The concept was to combine video conferencing with the intention of being publicly accessible and for the purpose of sharing knowledge and resources. The post I wrote explaining it was well received, and over 100 comments streamed in, offering encouragement and resources. A professor from Parsons (the New School for Design) reached out and offered to host the prototype on the New School server; a designer from Australia offered to put together a logo and user interface mockups; and other collaborators around the world jumped in to experiment with it together. In less than a month, Junto was born.

The next project that came about was a video called *The Future of Money*.[4] It started with an e-mail I received from the innovation leader at SWIFT, a global financial messaging network for banks and financial institutions. He was inspired by some things I had written about the true meaning of wealth and value, and the ideas I'd been laying out about the future of money and currency. He wanted me to come speak at SIBOS, a huge financial services conference that was to convene in Amsterdam.

Enter panic attack and imposter syndrome.

You have nothing to offer. Your ideas are silly. What do you know about finance? They're going to think you're a joke. You will fail.

My mind paralyzing me, I almost turned down the offer. But my friends, family and online community said, "Go for it!" So I thought, *What better way to express the emerging paradigm of a peer-to-peer, collaborative economy than to show how it works by example?*

I reached out to a video musician/designer team in Berlin and asked if they'd be interested in cocreating a video for the conference. They were stoked and even helped me find a great room to rent in their neighborhood, at a fraction of the price of a hotel room. They told me we could get interviews, editing and post-production done within two weeks.

I was both exhilarated and terrified.

Here I was, about to make a huge leap of faith: traveling to a foreign country to work on a time-sensitive project with people who were essentially strangers.

But this is how the new economy works, where trust can be built in a networked environment with peers around the planet. Through blogs, Twitter and video chats on Skype, we assessed each others' caliber and decided it was worth a shot to collaborate.

When that business flight landed in Berlin, I was greeted by Gabriel and Pati, an amazing couple and gracious hosts who immediately made me feel at home. Though I had the rented room they arranged for me, I ended up crashing many a night on their living room futon after an intensive work day on the project. We documented our activity those two weeks for the public to follow via video blogs and tweets.

We launched an online crowdfunding campaign to garner support from the public while we completed a project we had already committed to doing for free. We managed to raise around $6,000 in just a few weeks.

The presentation of the video at SIBOS went well and mined some enthusiasm about how our generation views money and wealth.[5] It even got mentions in *The Huffington Post* and *Fast Company*, and has received over 20K views on Vimeo to date.

That entire experience was a testament to the potential of this new emerging economy, where we can create new opportunities for ourselves and partnerships with people around the globe.

Finally, a few months ago, I completed my graduate degree. I've since teamed up with a group of collaborators on a new video series, *The Future of Facebook Project*.[6] We're pushing the distributed collaboration meme further by framing this project under the banner of "Open Foresight."[7] It's a methodology mashing up futures studies frameworks and open participation and media creation, with the intention of producing videos to raise awareness, spark dialogue and move us toward shared understanding and meaning.

We've already had a successful crowdfunding campaign for the project on Kickstarter[8] and also received funding from our first corporate patron, Innotribe.[9] We've done close to 30 interviews with incredible technologists, authors, futurists and business leaders. The videos are already set to be presented at three conferences later this year.

And now here I am, in April 2011, with a career that is emerging from a simple blog and the genuine desire to connect communities and amplify the work of change agents and mission-driven organizations. I wouldn't have believed this was possible a year ago.

Now it seems I've built a brand and can actually build on that foundation to generate an income for myself while also promoting this new paradigm of collaborative work and peer-to-peer culture. I've recently started writing a blog on Forbes.com, and was asked to contribute on CNN.com as well, giving me an outlet to spread the word to the mainstream. Businesses and organizations are starting to reach out to me for assistance with online community building, brand development and leaning how to communicate a message.

Now I see this life as an Epic Adventure, with each of us being the hero of our own personal mission. Here are three big insights I've had these past few years that make me confident in this belief:

- Your community already exists and is waiting for you.
- Your vision already exists—it is a shared one.
- The tools of empowerment already exist and are ready to be wielded.

The pieces you need really are there; they're just often hard to recognize. I went through a long phase of utter despair and hopelessness and had no idea how to move forward. Only after putting myself out there with authenticity and a beginner's mind did I see I was surrounded by a community of change agents with the heart, the vision and the capacity to act.

As we all move forward in building the kind of society we want to see and the lives we want to lead, we realize more and more that everything is interconnected and we can go further by connecting, collaborating and amplifying each other's efforts than by stubbornly trying to reinvent the wheel.

We're all in this together. Find your tribe and go change the world.

Organizing the Precariat

TOM JUDD

n the summer of 2009 I joined the approximately 4.4 million young people who were out of work and seeking a job during the Great Recession.[10] Having been laid off from a paid organizing position working with renters and with homeowners struggling with foreclosure, I was lucky enough to have an unemployment check to pay my student loans while I searched for work. During the fall I came into some luck—friends who worked for a major Washington, DC, nonprofit call center said they could get me a job. I would once again have the chance to do meaningful work while being able to pay the bills. They told me there were some issues around pay and treatment of workers, but I was ready for the challenge. As an anarchist, I believe in fighting where I stand—be it in the workplace, my home or my neighborhood—and I would be entering a hot workplace with a number of like-minded people.

What I encountered at the call center was similar to other nonprofits—an office filled with dedicated, capable young people who put up with low pay and no benefits in the name of making a difference. Most of the people I worked with were women in college or who had recently graduated. It's a high-stress job with a lot of second-hand emotional trauma from intense counseling with callers, low compensation and lack of respect, which have all led to high turnover in the past. Like a number of nonprofits I have worked for or observed, the supposedly social-justice–oriented call center made a name for itself by providing a service to people in need, while throwing workers under the bus and in the process exploiting both the needy and the employees. Important work was provided on the cheap by committed people willing to forgo things like good pay and benefits, which resulted in burnout. The dismal condition of the job market had pushed more workers to hold on to these jobs, however, which led to a stronger sense of community in the office.

I became involved in the incipient organizing effort, mostly observing as several strong, amazing women put time and effort into laying the groundwork for a union campaign—researching, making contacts, mapping the office for who might be interested and setting up meetings among those people. I would spend the next year alongside these inspiring women fighting for better wages, better working conditions and dignity on the job.

There was a lot to be unhappy about for the staff at our call center. Benefits were limited to case managers and others working full time, and periodic six-month raises had recently been eliminated. Contrary to DC law, we were not receiving sick leave. Wages for operators averaged between 9 and 10 dollars an hour, and working 40 hours a week was prohibited. These low wages and limited hours left many, including me, qualifying for food stamps and Medicaid and contending with DC's extremely expensive housing market. Recent college graduates often have the added burden of paying student loans. All of these factors led more than a few to make the call center a second job while they worked elsewhere.

In a very unpopular move that further angered workers, management removed Internet access from operators' computers as collective punishment for one person's supposed misuse. Case managers, however, retained Internet access, a clear double standard in trust and respect. A threat was then issued that "too much" talking with fellow workers on the job (call-related or otherwise) would be punished (an action that further proved that management was out of touch with the realities of working at a crisis call center). Other staff positions in the organization were well compensated, and many of the people who held them were often dismissive or disrespectful toward hotline staff.

Hierarchy was as much present in the call center as in any private organization, and there was a strong inequality between those who managed and those who worked. Changes on the hotline, big or small, were implemented with little or no consultation with employees. The manager of the hotline would waste staff time by using employees as a sounding board for her personal issues, and case managers would have to fill in for her during frequent absences. The executive director ruled by decree—no matter how bad or petty her decisions were, she was accountable only to herself. She bragged about the hotline in public, but she didn't know the names of anyone who worked there, including the person who had worked there the longest. When discontent was voiced, management responded with either threats or pleas to cheer up.

As frustration levels for staff at the hotline continued to rise, operators held meetings outside of work to talk about how to respond to the Internet situation. When workers felt unappreciated, we held get-togethers. Our preliminary organizing efforts, ranging from clandestine e-mails to workplace meetings, were initially met with indifference by the bosses.

As our efforts gained momentum, pressure continued to build. After several months of organizing, our little impromptu committee was weighing whether to formalize and start a union drive in earnest. The decision to reach out to a union was not a simple one. Supporters of unionizing argued that it would be the best way for us to have resources and support for our struggle. However, we encountered and experienced a certain amount of skepticism, pessimism and, most frequently, ignorance about what a union would mean for the hotline. There was also hesitation to risk unionizing, understanding that we could lose our jobs if that word was connected with us. While these discussions were happening, however, we did not anticipate the coming reaction from management.

Faced with an office infected by "low morale" and discontent that did not rapidly disappear on its own, the executive director and her cronies launched a massive management counteroffensive designed to kill the sickness through a form of management kindness. An official but anonymous survey was issued with the declared intent to figure out what workers were unhappy about. Plenty of room was allowed for us to voice our concerns, with the eventual promise that the executive director would read them all. Action on some of the grievances was also implied, instilling some hope in disgruntled staffers. After a few weeks, management rolled out a laundry list of changes culled from the survey. Some, such as restoring the Internet and implementing modest raises for operators, were intended to appease unhappy workers and smother discontent. Along with these incentives, however, was a restructuring plan that would replace most daytime hours for operators with salaried, full-time positions. Unhappy workers could either buy in or be squeezed out.

The organizing effort was effectively killed off with this sort of kindness. Most of the organizing committee applied for and received promotions to positions that gave them higher wages and kept them busy with new responsibilities. Operators who had remained after months of mistreatment began quitting or scaling back their hours. Now daytime hours are almost filled with full-time operators, all but two of whom have never worked there before. The previous sense of community was destroyed as workers were isolated and their hours disrupted by new, full-time hires. In the face of this restructuring, part-timers were left scrambling to keep their jobs.

We now know that this is a common tactic among the anti-union sector—with analogies comparing organizers to mosquitoes, management suggests "draining the swamp" of workplace grievances and issues that motivate the organizing in order to kill the "disease" of unionizing. It was bitterly ironic to those who knew that the same executive director who was using these tactics had been employed as a high-level union organizer earlier in her career.

In spite of its failure, our effort to organize our workplace was worthwhile. The conditions on the hotline, combined with what we perceived as a critical mass of people interested in changing them, demanded we do something, and we responded to the call. While the failure of these efforts was due in large part to the boss and her actions, our own mistakes are important to note as well. One major issue we contended with was the high turnover of organizers. What originated as regular six- to ten-person meetings of people who had worked in the office for a year or more became three- or four-person meetings of newer folks, including me, as other people either left their jobs or, more often, fell away because they felt self-conscious about organizing while they were not in the worst positions at work. Case managers and assistant case managers wanted to step aside to make room for operators to lead, but most of them simply stopped attending meetings altogether. In addition, valid issues raised early on in the process around the organization's lack of inclusiveness and leadership from people of color on the hotline were never fully addressed, and when they were raised, many people reacted by pulling back from organizing altogether.

Furthermore, I don't think we as a committee armed ourselves with enough knowledge or strategized enough about how to organize our workplace. The idea of "organizer training" had been discussed very early on, but for a number of reasons never came together. The people most involved in the organizing, including me, were also slow and more than a little hesitant to expand that circle, in part because we didn't know how and also because of the risk involved. Some of the basic organizing practices that we were encouraged to use—such as creating a formal list of e-mails and phone numbers—were done but not shared with our contact in the labor movement, thus creating difficulty in moving the process forward.

I would also argue that we didn't have enough guidance from the people we contacted in the labor movement. None of us had organized a workplace before and, while we were provided with a fair amount of knowledge about unions in general, more solid ideas of what organizing could have looked like as well as best practices used by successful campaigns would have been very helpful. A full- or part-time organizer working with us on a regular basis may also have helped—not to do the organizing for us, but to check in with us and throw around ideas, make suggestions, etc.

Young workers get a rough deal in this economy. The skyrocketing cost of college has left many of us deeply in debt, and the well-paying jobs with which to pay it off are few and far between, demanding years of work experience or higher (and more expensive) degrees. Benefits are often shoddy or out of reach for entry-level positions such as those on the hotline, and job security is weak or nonexistent. (I've worked three entry-level jobs in the three years since I graduated.) This leaves many young people bouncing from job to job and often either not invested enough in the job to want to change it for the better or so concerned about the idea of losing it that they don't want to risk standing up against unfair conditions.

The nonprofit industrial complex is also at fault in many ways. In an economy where the remnants of the US welfare state are shrinking, nonprofits have increased both in number and size. They claim the responsibility of aiding the people who are losing in the economy, yet at the same time, funding to these organizations remains limited and the conditions for money are dictated by powerful foundations. An unfortunate reality of limited funding may mean limited wages and benefits for those working at an organization. However, as the situation on the hotline illustrates, nonprofits will often be just as unfair to their workers as their private sector counterparts. Caring, socially minded young people attracted by the promise that their jobs will make a difference and be meaningful may put up with poor working conditions for years because they prioritize the work over themselves, and management uses this to its advantage. Meanwhile, executive directors and staff higher in the hierarchy will pull in hundreds of thousands of dollars, with full benefits packages on top.

How long will those temporary changes, rearrangements and concessions that defeated organizing at the call center last? Part-time operators are still underpaid and lack benefits. There is now greater inequality, as people doing the same work are treated very differently. The culture of the hotline has been uprooted for the most part, and management remains unaccountable and free to do as it pleases. However, the restructured hotline is already deteriorating, as three full-timers have left in the past few months. Full-timer operator pay is higher than that for a part-time operator, but not high enough for much retention of workers, and operators feel the stress of unfair overtime rules. Even as many people have left and some of the more rebellious workers have advanced in the hierarchy, there are still workers there who participated in the struggle. The seeds of discontent remain; it's a question of when they will surface again.

How to Start
A Worker Co-Op
MIRA LUNA

n the age of unemployment, downsizing and outsourcing,
where can a poor soul find a job? Well, maybe it's time we
create our own. Self-employment is an option and can
seem freeing, but it's hard to do everything yourself and
find time for a non-work life. The worker co-op is an alternative to the isolation of self-employment and the exploi-
tation of traditional jobs.

Worker co-ops can be more satisfying than working
for the man. Worker-owners aren't forced into a hierarchy,
and they have more say over what the business does than
traditional employees. You still have to be responsible managing a co-op—maybe more so—but your coworker-owners
will likely be nicer and more understanding of personal
needs and quirks than middle-management at any corporation. You will probably make more money by cutting out
the investors and managers, unless you were one of them,
in which case: welcome to egalitarianism! In typical low-
paying industries, worker-owners can make several times
what they were pulling in as employees. For example, in
Petaluma, California, Alvarado Street Bakery worker-owners
take home around $60,000 a year—a hell of a lot better than
working for minimum wage. As a worker-owner, you are less
likely to get laid off, both because co-ops prioritize steady
employment over short-term profits and because they are
more sustainable than their conventional counterparts.

So what is a worker co-op? It's an enterprise owned and
democratically controlled by its workers. There are endless

variations on co-ops, which means there are many questions to consider before forming your own unique venture. Remember, you are starting a real business, not a hippie commune! If you've never started a business before, you will need support—read up on how to start a firm; get advice from co-op development organizations (listed below); and talk to co-op-friendly lawyers and accountants. You will need a business plan, co-op-specific legal incorporation documents and capital to finance you in the beginning. Additionally, you will want an organization plan detailing how you will run your co-op cooperatively.

One of the first barriers to starting a worker cooperative is finding others willing to be part of the initiating group. If you are working at a business that wants to be converted to a co-op (whether the managers know it or not), you may already have your members. To find new folks, it may be helpful to send an announcement to any work-related e-mail list (such as for groups interested in food justice, hackers and even hippie communes) and post flyers at related businesses or job assistance centers in your area. Invite people to a meeting for your new enterprise, or better yet, hold a general co-op matchmaker start-up fair where people can meet, get to know each other and discuss first steps. Invite existing co-ops to offer initial advice, then set up an e-mail list or wiki that helps people find each other by posting new co-op opportunities on an ongoing basis. Some worker cooperative development organizations listed below can help with this.

Once you've gathered your initiating group, here are some questions to consider when forming a worker co-op:
- What is your common goal and purpose—fair employment for people of color, access to healthy food, sustainability, independent media, selling locally produced

goods? Identifying this will make decision-making easier and get you through the tough times.

- Are you forming a new business or converting an old one? If it's new, is there a market for your service or product? Do you have a niche? What is your expertise? Being a co-op gives you a leg up, but you still must provide a needed product or service that competes in the greater, cutthroat capitalist marketplace—until it collapses. If it's a drowning business, is the owner willing to sell? And how will you save the business? You may need to make major changes to make it sustainable.
- Who will be on your team? It helps to have people in your crew with experience in your product or service, people skills (communication, meeting facilitation, decision-making) and skills in running the different parts of a business (management, accounting, marketing, etc.) or at least friendly consultants on hand to do these things. Your team needs to really be into the co-op model, even if they learn the details later. Remember that you will be making a long-term commitment to spending 40+ hours together weekly, depending on each other for survival, making major decisions together and caring for each other. (That sounds like marriage!)
- How will new worker owners join? Trial periods are highly recommended. Think dating, engagement, then marriage—no need to rush. Some co-ops have a buy-in requirement to become an official owner. This can be in an initial lump-sum investment, periodic deductions from paychecks or sweat equity contribution to demonstrate serious long-term commitment and give equal power. Training new worker-owners to run the business as a cooperative is crucial—people are often trained in the business world to compete, control and manipulate,

not cooperate or communicate. On the other hand, people who are into cooperation often don't have business skills or work-specific expertise. Your team really needs both.

- How will you manage your co-op—collectively, with rotating representative managers, professional hired managers? Usually big co-ops have more hierarchy and job divisions. Small co-ops tend to collectively manage and pitch in to run the different parts of a business. There is no one way, but democracy rules. Disguised and non-consensual hierarchies, however, can be particularly damaging to morale.

- Who will make decisions? And when and how—consensus, super-majority, majority? It helps to clarify the process in detail and delegate minor or certain types of decisions to individuals or committees so you don't spend too much time in meetings. Believe me, long, indecisive meetings have killed more co-ops than the financial crisis. On the other hand, transparency, inclusion and frequent communication maintain the cohesiveness and trust of the group. Consensus works in small groups that get along and have a lot in common. In bigger, more diverse groups, it can create enough inertia and conflict to stifle a business. I like using modified consensus (try to get everyone's enthusiastic agreement if possible) and super-majorities as a good middle path. The key here is not voting-rule dogma but developing a communication process that allows everyone to be heard and resolves disputes fairly.

- How much money will you need? Where will you get funding—from your new worker-owners, a loan from the former owner, a loan from a bank (try one that has lent to co-ops successfully) or a grant for worker co-op start-ups? Be realistic about your budget—people may

SHARE or DIE

be leaving their lifeline paycheck, and you need to make sure you have enough funds for everyone to make it until the business becomes profitable—or nonprofitable if that's your bag. One failed co-op can give them all a bad rap.

Whew! That sounds like a lot of work. But worker-owners I've talked to say in the long run it's totally worth it. To help you get started, some resources are listed below, including worker co-op development organizations. Starting a new co-op can create jobs, not just for you but also for people who may have never had the opportunity to own a business or earn a living wage. Worker co-ops are part of a larger movement to create an economy that is democratic and just and takes care of everyone. And it can start with you and your coworkers.

Reading resources

- Worker Cooperative Toolbox (bit.ly/wynewg)
- Steps to Starting a Worker Co-op (bit.ly/yPmWDs)
- A Technology Freelancer's Guide to Starting a Worker Cooperative (bit.ly/Mo5ih)

Worker co-op development organizations

- US Federation of Worker Cooperatives (usworker.coop)
- California Center for Cooperative Development (cccd .coop)
- National Cooperative Business Association (ncba.coop)
- Network of Bay Area Worker Cooperatives (in the SF Bay Area) (nobawc.org)

Get on the Lattice
ASTRI VON ARBIN AHLANDER
and YELIZAVETTA KOFMAN

When the class of 2012 throw their caps in the air, most won't have job offers waiting for them. Instead, many graduates will prepare to move back home with their parents, to take yet another unpaid internship or to accept any old job that will help pay off their student loans.

The bubbles burst

It was an entirely different scene when we graduated from Middlebury College on May 27, 2007. On that day, the Dow Jones was at a high of 13,507 points, and climbing. Bill Clinton, the commencement speaker, gently reminded us to be mindful of people in our society and around the world who haven't been blessed with the many gifts we had been given ("the gift of a fine mind, the gift of a chance to be here, the gift of all the choices you have when you leave"). We tried our best at humility while taking in his grave, important words, but it was hard to contain the aura of invincibility and optimism in the air. The world was ours for the conquering. And in just a short while, many of our classmates were going to cash in their college credentials for real world currency: entry-level jobs.

The most praised of our peers were heading into lucrative corporate jobs as management consultants, bankers, analysts and paralegals. They were going to work for prestigious firms in exciting cities: McKinsey in Boston, Sullivan & Cromwell in New York, J.P. Morgan in London. Quite a few of our classmates signed on with Lehman Brothers. (Dick Fuld, the company's CEO, was also listening to Bill Clinton speak on that intermittently rainy day in May—his son was graduating too.) As at most selective institutions that year, post-college chatter centered around signing bonuses and apartment-hunting plans.

And then there were the two of us. We were despondent. Neither of us had a job. This was over a year and a half before the sudden collapse of Lehman Brothers and the financial meltdown, so there were plenty of jobs out there. We had opportunities; we just hadn't signed on any dotted line. So why the graduation-day sulking?

For starters, we were grossly underwhelmed by what we thought were our post-college choices: under-stimulating corporate jobs leading to law or business school and, many billable hours and first-class red-eyes later, financial success. Or some other kind of job, in the arts or at a nonprofit perhaps, that would be poorly paid and probably administrative anyway. Going corporate was the sure bet—and the difference between the sure thing and anything else felt huge in terms of future earnings and respect. Besides, corporate was pretty much the only thing on the menu at our career services office, whose posted job openings read like a list of the Fortune 500. The jobs our families and our schools pointed us toward struck us as homogeneous and lifeless, and we wondered why that was.

The other reason for our despondency was that we had inadvertently stumbled into uncharted territory for college students, openly questioning how our future careers would fit in with our future family lives. It started out innocently enough: we were lounging in the sunshine with some girlfriends who, like us, were only days away from graduation. Apropos of the future, a popular topic, we asked our friends what they thought they would do when they had children. At first, they seemed confused. Could we clarify? We guessed that we could, though our question had been spontaneous; at this point we weren't yet armed with questionnaires. What would they do about their jobs when they had children—how would they make it work? We had expected answers involving words like "sharing," "flexibility" or maybe even "sheer force of will." Instead, our friends' nearly uniform response was a fumbling explanation that they guessed they would take a couple of years off working. As in quitting? As in being stay-at-home moms? What?

These friends of ours were intelligent, educated and ambitious young women. None of them spoke about quitting with unequivocal enthusiasm but rather with a reluctant sense of necessity. Never would we have thought our peers considered their options so limited. The crux seemed to be that most of these women (all of them middle or upper-middle class, in their early twenties) had been raised with stay-at-home mothers, and all of them believed that a parent staying home full time was the ideal childcare arrangement for young children. But why didn't a single one of them mention the father of these future children when they talked about finding a way to balance their professional and personal lives? Why did they seem to think it was their burden to bear alone?

Riled up after our alarming lawn conversation, we tracked down some of our male friends and posed the same question to them: how did they expect to balance work and kids? Their responses were comically vague. The most common reference was to Little League, whatever that had to do with anything.

Then we asked some established professionals—mostly older alumni and friends of our parents—what would happen to an employee who took a few years of leave, and they told us such a move would likely stop a high-level career in its tracks. We poked around on the Internet and discovered that no American employer was going to grant a few years of parental leave anyway—they weren't required to provide any at all, and the very best offered at most a couple of months, often to women only.

What started with a few questions about combining parenthood with a career snowballed into more and more questions about the day-to-day of corporate work culture in America—about flexibility (mostly rhetoric), about face time (ubiquitous), about sick leave (not guaranteed) and about vacation (an average of ten days for the first five years).

As we contemplated our first post-undergraduate step, we suddenly felt like all the air had been let out of our balloon—our inflated collegiate egos a fine metaphor for the nation's economy, we would soon discover. The new picture of working life that emerged was nothing like the one we had imagined. We thought we were going to have rocket careers, happy children, and passionate, supportive partners with stellar careers of their own. But when we tried to break all this down, it just didn't add up. When, exactly, were we supposed to have children if 25 to 40 was when we had to prove ourselves at work? How were we supposed to bring up kids if we and our spouses both worked 50 hours a week?

We tried tinkering with various scenarios. What if you and your spouse work part time while your kids are young, and then ratchet back up a few years later (you'll have decades to catch up, after all)? No, we were told that scaling back, even for a short time, signals to employers that you're not serious about your career, that you're not interested in making partner, for example. Part time wasn't even an option in many jobs. But we do want to make partner! So do our friends, men and women alike! This work system was all wrong! As we prepared to receive our diplomas, we couldn't shake the feeling that the game was rigged from the start.

Of course, our initial rock-star-by-30 outlook was incredibly naive—but admit it, you had similarly rosy expectations. Which leads us to another major realization we had: our generation has a very poor sense of the options and limitations we're likely to face, and how best to prepare for the work-life gauntlet. This is shocking considering how easily and routinely we research every other aspect of our lives (closest Thursday night happy hour, cheapest flight to Kuala Lumpur, best hairdresser in a five-mile radius, etc.).

We found our collective cluelessness so surprising, and so disturbing, that we decided to do some research about how our generation, the so-called Generation Y, really sees the challenging dance move that is the work-life balance. We spent the year after graduation asking other college students and recent grads about what they were hoping for, professionally and personally, and how they planned to achieve their goals. We traveled to New York, Madrid, Paris, Stockholm and Moscow. We found interview subjects in bars and parks and online. We drank coffee in every café in Paris and beer in smoky, underground members' clubs in Moscow.

That's right, it was a pretty tough life. We told our sponsors that this Grand Tour was about giving other young people the information we wish we'd had before graduating college, but really it was about blind self-interest. We were terrified. We figured we could at least learn from other people's mistakes before we messed up our own lives. Maybe we could even help other Gen Yers in the process.

What we didn't anticipate was that less than a year after we ditched our first job offers for tape recorders, a global financial crisis would spark a level of debate beyond our wildest dreams. We now live in critical times. The financial crisis in America and the consequent fallout constitute a potential paradigm shift. Suddenly, everything is up for debate. With men bearing the brunt of the lay-offs, and taking it very hard, society at large is starting to question whether it's healthy for one person to shoulder the financial well-being of an entire family. With women becoming the sole breadwinners in more and more families, the question of why women earn less than men—and what can be done about it—has new urgency. With people losing their jobs, and the benefits that come with those jobs, we're starting to question whether an employer-based benefit system makes sense when a rapidly growing fraction of the workforce are freelancers and independent contractors. With finance disgraced, young people are wondering what careers will bring them respect and fulfillment. Tighter budgets have forced us, as individuals and as a nation, to think about what is really important. We're at a point of transition. The question is: which direction should we go?

Our answer is simple: get on the lattice or die.

The corporate ladder

What the hell is a lattice? Bear with us for a bit. Surely, you've heard the term "the corporate ladder." To succeed in a career you have to climb up the well-defined rungs of a ladder: up, up, up, until—nope, just up.

The corporate ladder is a wonderfully clear visual—it's also the epitome of inflexibility. There are really only two directions you can go on a ladder: up or down. There's little room for sidesteps or pauses, let alone for backtracks. Consider a Harvard study that surveyed alumni 15 years after graduation. It estimated the average financial penalty for someone who took a year and a half off and then returned to work. In medicine, that person earned 16 percent less than a similar doctor who had not taken time off, and that's actually the lowest penalty—so keep at it pre-meds. For graduates who didn't get a graduate degree, the gap was 25 percent.

For lawyers and PhDs it was about 29 percent. And for people who work in finance and consulting, it was a whopping 41 percent. And that's for taking one and a half years off. Not the two or three that our smart, ambitious girlfriends were talking about. Fifty-nine percent of an average finance salary is still a large chunk of change, even today, but it means that taking one and a half years off puts you on a completely different track than the worker who managed, somehow, to stay on the ladder.

We might be okay with the inflexibility of the ladder model if we were guaranteed stability in exchange. That was the deal in past decades: workers were often rewarded with a stable career and a gold watch at the end of a lifetime of loyal employment. But the working world we enter now looks very different from the one our parents entered then. The rungs of the ladder are not given; the ladder may in fact end, abruptly, after years of dedicated investment.

The reasons for the demise of the corporate ladder model are complex, but at the most basic level it comes down to flexibility. Our globalized, competitive world demands flexibility. Employers want to be fluid, hiring and firing with the market's increasingly fickle whims. For all the benefits of a ladder career in terms of stability and institutionalized knowledge, it's just not flexible. So in the long run, it's out.

What's more, the ladder career works for only a tiny fraction of the workforce—the ever-elusive "ideal worker." The ideal worker can work all the time, year-round, and has few responsibilities outside of work. Guess what? The ideal worker is a man—a man with a stay-at-home wife to take care of everything else. Perhaps our readers snicker at such a dated idea, but when you look at the corporate ladder world, it's not set up for individuals to deal with family and personal responsibilities—things like taking care of a sick parent or picking up your kids from school or even having kids for that matter! Never mind that the ideal worker model is a recipe for a heart attack. Never mind that in the past 30 years there has been a momentous increase in dual-earner households and single-parent families. Never mind that today the majority of college graduates are women. Companies still expect that a man with a stay-at-home wife will show up at the office.

Even if men still wanted to shoulder the financial burdens of their families alone and women were dying to give up their careers to tend the hearth and all that, the *Mad Men* set up just isn't a possibility for 98 percent of us anymore. Most families need two breadwinners to pay the bills these days. That's the 21st-century reality.

So, what is life like for dual-earner families in a corporate ladder world? First of all, get ready to put in a whole lot of hours. Over the past 25 years, the combined weekly work hours of dual-earner couples with children under 18 at home has increased by an average 10 hours per week, from 81 to 91 hours. At the same time, with anxiety about the future and getting into college at an all-time high, parenting has actually become more intensive. But the majority of employers still expect their employees to act as though they have no other responsibilities outside the office. It's downright taboo to use a family commitment as an excuse in a work setting—it may be superficially accepted, but it'll "mommy-track" you faster than you can say "Baby Björn."

The US government has been pathetically slow to respond to the changes in our society. Here's a shocker: the US is one of only four countries in the world—and we're talking about the whole world, not just developed countries—that doesn't guarantee some form of paid parental leave. The other three countries are Papa New Guinea, Lesotho and Swaziland. Under the Family and Medical Leave Act, employers in the United States have to offer 12 weeks of unpaid parental leave, but that applies only to employers with over 50 employees. More importantly, who can afford to take unpaid leave? Workers aren't even guaranteed any paid sick leave or vacation. In the 2011 study, "Failing its Families: Lack of Paid Leave and Work-Family Supports in the US," Human Rights Watch calls a spade a spade: the situation for American families today is a human rights violation.

To give you some perspective, out of the top 20 economies in the world, 18 guarantee their workers at least 30 days of paid vacation. In Sweden, new parents have 18 months of paid parental leave, which they can split as they see fit and with 2 months reserved for the father. Sweden also guarantees unlimited days to take care of sick children. Yes, Sweden's family policies are exceptional, but America's stand out as being exceptionally bad.

Are we freaking you out? Don't panic. We're not going to lie to you: it is scary out there. And despite reading countless books and reports and articles on these issues, we haven't come across one magic cure-all. The best antidote to the inflexible ladder culture we've found is embracing and pushing for a whole new culture: a lattice culture.

What is a lattice culture?

A lattice looks like several ladders combined into a sort of web. On a lattice, the possible path is not simply up or down like it is on a ladder. You can choose to move up, down, diagonally, or sideways. A lattice allows you to pause, to slow down, to switch jobs and fields more freely than a ladder does. The lattice is the model for a career track characterized by flexibility. And, ultimately, it is a model that takes into account the reality of modern workers. It means you wouldn't have to completely get off track to fulfill your personal commitments or adventures.

Sounds great. But how do we get there?

The truth is that it's going to take serious changes to our current ladder culture, especially to the way we as a society think about work and career building, for a lattice lifestyle to be possible for a significant chunk of people. We're not there yet. Not even close. That said, there is hope. There are people out there in the US who, despite all odds, are successfully leading a lattice-like lifestyle. For example, bloggers Amy and Mark Vachon have recently come out with a book that is full of couples who rearranged their lives to make a lattice lifestyle work. Often this involves both partners asking employers to go part time or to have flextime. Flextime means you work the same amount of hours, but you choose your own start and end times. It enables you to work four-day weeks, for example.

We have to be honest with you. These kinds of arrangements are not possible for everyone. We talked to a computer programmer in Moscow who told his employer he would like to work from 7 to 3, instead of 9 to 5. His services were highly valued, the company had an accommodating outlook, and his employer agreed. On the other hand, a TV producer we talked to in New York asked his employer for extra vacation days instead of a raise and the employer flat out said, "Nope, against company policy." Not all employers are going to be agreeable.

Switching to a lattice lifestyle, even if your employer is willing, also means readjusting your expectations. You really can't have it all, all the time. A flexible lattice lifestyle will probably mean that you earn less money, at least for a time. If you want to be the CEO of Coca Cola by the time you're 35, you can stop reading right now. It's not going to happen. We realize that someone has to be the CEO of Coca Cola. For now, that person is probably going to be a man with a stay-at-home wife. It's true: 97 percent of Fortune 500 CEOs are men. Of the female CEOs, only 30 percent have children. But this doesn't have to be the case in the future. There are alternatives, even at the very top.

Take job-sharing, which we learned about while talking to a newspaper editor in Sweden. He shares his position with another person. When he went on paternity leave, the newspaper wasn't left scrambling, because the top position wasn't in the hands of just one person. They were prepared. Another alternative we heard about was hiring temporary workers to fill in for those on leave; this way younger workers can cut their teeth in a position with real responsibilities and the company can have a test run to see if they are worth hiring full time.

In Europe, especially in Scandinavia, whole societies are increasingly working together to make a lattice culture possible. The government guarantees generous leaves and employers support these leaves with their own, internal policies. In France, freelancers pay into an unemployment fund, so that when they experience gaps in employment they too have a safety net.

In the US, we're still scrambling. We still live in a ladder world. But in a society where gold watches and 40 years in one company are rarities rather than norms, where female labor force participation and changing masculine expectations break down the model of the ideal worker, where people jump from job to job, and perhaps from field to field, where innovation and risk-taking are key to success, the ladder is outdated. The lattice is the present and future.

It would be nice if all of society recognized this, because we can achieve so much more together than we can as mere individuals. It's asking a lot for you alone to make demands of an indifferent employer, compared to having new national policies to back you up. Without a doubt, the US needs employment reform: universal health care, paid parental leave, sick leave and vacation policies would be a good start.

But until our society gets its act together and offers workers and families those basic building blocks of a lattice lifestyle, individuals are going to have to make it work themselves. There is no blueprint for this. But after researching the hell out of these questions, and interviewing students as well as young and seasoned professionals for hours upon hours, we've come up with some basic advice.

How to get on the lattice

1. Become educated about the realities of the workplace and the career you would like for yourself. You should do this early, preferably while you're still in college, but it's never too late. Research the hours and conditions required of the particular career you're interested in and weigh that against what you want for your personal life. As work–life balance crusader Nigel Marsh said in his 2011 TED (Technology, Entertainment & Design) talk, "Certain jobs and career paths are fundamentally incompatible with being meaningfully engaged on a day-to-day basis with a young family." Think corporate law, management consulting, investment banking, CEOdom. Be realistic. Talk to people you admire. Don't just ask them about what graduate school they went to and how they got their first job. Ask them about the challenges; ask them about how they balance their work and family lives practically and emotionally. You may not love what you hear, but you'll learn.

2. Decide what is really important to you—whether it's being geographically mobile, working in the outdoors, having control over your time, being in a position of power, being a very present part of your children's lives

or living lavishly. Be honest with yourself. Make sure you know what it is you want so that you don't find yourself, ten years down the line, with a life that doesn't fit you. Again, be realistic. If having a flexible schedule is high on your list, for example, come to terms with the fact that you may not be able to have a professional career that gives you a great deal of managerial power. If you want to be a very hands-on parent, don't count on being able to balance that with a 60-hours-a-week gig.

3. Talk openly with your partner early on about all the tricky stuff—what you expect from one another, who's going to do what and earn what. It can be a pretty awkward conversation to have, but it's necessary if you're going to be serious about somebody. Love works in mysterious ways, but love may not be enough if you find out, too far down the line, that your spouse has wildly different expectations when it comes to division of responsibilities at home.

4. Don't be afraid to ask. Do your research, make a good case, and you may be surprised how much your employer will be willing to accommodate. You create value, and employers really are loath to lose a solid worker. Workplace culture can change. But it will take a critical mass of employees demanding more flexibility. Let's each take one for the team, Gen Y.

To conclude: know what you want. Find out what a certain career will demand of you and how that weighs against your personal goals. Make sure you and your future partner are on the same page as soon as possible. Most of all, pause in the rush to excel that you're caught up in, and ask yourself the important questions: What kinds of hours and working conditions come with the particular career I'm thinking of pursuing? What kind of standard of living do I want to have? What do I expect from a partner? What does he or she expect from me?

It's a mistake we all tend to make, skipping over the tough questions, because, well, they're hard. But, remember, articulating the question is the first important step toward finding the answer.

The Gen Y Guide to Collaborative Consumption
BETH BUCZYNSKI

When our parents graduated from college, the bachelor's degree was a coveted badge of honor. It gave applicants instant cred (and usually a larger paycheck) no matter what the job. Now having a bachelor's degree does nothing to make an applicant stand out from the masses. And if you're applying for a job well below your skill level because you're desperate for a paycheck, that B.S. degree will probably get your carefully crafted résumé tossed in the trash."

American youth are slowly realizing that the old system is broken and no longer holds the answer to all their dreams and desires. We're discovering that stable, satisfying careers can be found outside the offices and factories around which our parents and grandparents built their lives. We're acknowledging that the pursuit of bigger, better and faster things have plunged our country into a time of despair and difficulty. We're convinced that business as usual isn't an option any longer—but what's the alternative?

Together, we're learning that instead of waiting for politicians and corporations to fix the system, it's possible to create a better one of our own, right under their noses—a new way of living, in which access is valued over ownership, experience is valued over material possessions, and "mine" becomes "ours" so everyone's needs are met without waste.[12]

If these ideas get your blood pumping, there's good news: young people all over the world are already making them a reality. It's called collaborative consumption[13] (or the sharing economy[14]), and it's changing the way we work, play and interact with each other. It's fueled by the instant connection and communication of the Internet, yet it's manifesting itself in interesting ways offline too.[15]

If you're ready to connect with people who can help you save money, pursue your passions and reduce waste, here's a quick-start guide to your sharing experience:

1. **Remove all items from the box and assess.**

   Sit down with yourself (or some friends) and talk about what you've got, what you need and what you could live without. Take stock of what you'd be willing to share,[16] rent or give away. Write down all the things you really need to be productive/happy/connected. Then, cross out all the things that you want just for the sake of having them, and highlight all the things that involve a valuable experience. Now you have a list you can tackle through sharing.

2. **Connect to the power source.**

   The collaborative consumption movement[17] empowers people to thrive despite the economic climate. Instead of looking to the government or corporations to tell us what we want or to create a solution for our problems, we take action to meet our own needs in a creative fashion. This is our power source. Start looking for ways to share at school, on community billboards, by asking friends or by using the resources below.

Housing

- **Roommates.com** (roommates.com): A roommate search service, such as this, which covers thousands of cities nationwide, is very useful.

- **How to Start a Housing Co-op** (bit.ly/gH1SWA): This is one of the best affordable-housing options around, and shared food expenses and cooking can increase your savings.
- **Guide to Sharing a House** (bit.ly/5wRHjO): Buying a home by yourself may be out of reach in high-cost areas, but shared ownership might be the ticket.
- **Cohousing Directory** (cohousing.org/directory): Cohousing is home ownership in a neighborhood that shares.
- **Craigslist** (craigslist.org/about/sites): Find almost anything, including a house or housemate, on Craigslist.

Social Food

- **Eat With Me** (eatwithme.net), **Grub With Us** (grubwithus.com) and **Gobble.com** (gobble.com) are the meals equivalent of Airbnb.com. Use them to find or host a meal in your neighborhood. Never eat alone!
- **MamaBake** (mamabake.com): Large-batch group cooking saves time and money, not to mention it's fun!
- **Local Harvest** (localharvest.org): This massive directory can help you find farmers' markets, Community Supported Agriculture (CSAs) and other sources of sustainably grown food in your area.
- **Neighborhood Fruit** (neighborhoodfruit.com): Find and offer free fruit to your neighbors with this site and iPhone app.

Personal Finance

- **Lending Club** (lendingclub.com/home.action): This online financial community brings together creditworthy borrowers and savvy investors so that both can benefit financially.
- **Zopa** (uk.zopa.com/ZopaWeb): When people get

together to lend and borrow money directly with each other, they can often sidestep the banks for a better deal.

- **Prosper** (prosper.com): This peer-to-peer lending site allows people to invest in each other in a way that is financially and socially rewarding.
- **SmartyPig** (smartypig.com): A social savings bank enables you to save for specific goals and engage friends and family to contribute.

Entrepreneurship/Work

- **Kickstarter** (kickstarter.com): This crowdfunding site is powered by a unique all-or-nothing funding method where projects must be fully funded or no money changes hands.
- **BetterMeans** (bettermeans.com/front/index.html): Use open-source decision-making rules and self-organizing principles to run your real-world projects.
- **Task Rabbit** (taskrabbit.com): This service that enables you to outsource your tasks and deliveries is available only in Boston and the San Francisco Bay area—for now.
- **Coworking Wiki** (bit.ly/AqRRJr), **Loosecubes** (loosecubes.com) or **Liquidspace** (liquidspace.com): Use these sites to find a friendly place to cowork. Coworking is a flexible and community-oriented workspace option for business travelers, independent workers and entrepreneurs.
- **A Guide to Casual Coworking** (bit.ly/hJlQrd): Why not cowork anywhere? Here's the definitive guide.

Travel

- **CouchSurfing** (couchsurfing.org): This is an international network that connects travelers with locals in over 230 countries and territories around the world with free accommodations and cultural exchange.

- **AirBnB** (airbnb.com): People who have space to spare connect here with those who are looking for a place to stay, all over the world.
- **Roomorama** (roomorama.com): Find short-term rentals all over the world through this online marketplace.
- **Tripping** (tripping.com): Tripping enables you to connect safely with locals who will introduce you to their towns, their cultures, their lives and their friends. Features ways of finding accommodations through trust networks such as university alumni associations.
- **How To Swap Cities** (bit.ly/yX4aed): Inspired by **SwapYourShop** (swapyourshop.com), this is a guide on how to swap offices with someone from another city.

Land/Gardening

- **HyperLocavore** (hyperlocavore.ning.com): Share yards, seeds, tools and good times growing food at this US-based garden sharing site!
- **Shared Earth** (sharedearth.com): Get free access to land and grow what you love; share some of the produce with the land owner and keep the rest. This is a US-based site.
- **Tool libraries** (bit.ly/ojw8): Check out this handy directory of tool libraries.
- **Landshare** (landshare.net): This UK-based service connects those who have land to share with those who need land for cultivating food.
- **How to start a Crop Mob** (bit.ly/AxyByN): Crop mobs allow you to get and give gardening help.

Transportation

- **Carsharing directory** (carsharing.net/where.html): Find car sharing service providers in your area with this international list.
- **Zimride** (public.zimride.com), **eRideShare** (erideshare .com): Find a ride or offer a ride on these top US-based ride-sharing platforms.
- **Carpooling.com** (carpooling.com): This is the largest ride-sharing community in Europe.
- **Park at myHouse** (parkatmyhouse.com/uk): Property-owners provide affordable and fine-free parking by renting their empty driveways, garages, car parks, etc. to drivers needing somewhere to park.
- **ZipCar** (zipcar.com): This is the largest fleet-based car sharing service in the world.
- **RelayRides** (relayrides.com), **Getaround** (getaround .com) and **Just Share It** (bit.ly/yJ97ea): Rent cars to or from neighbors using these US-based leaders of the peer-to-peer car-sharing movement. Available in select locations
- **WhipCar** (whipcar.com): This is a UK-based peer-to-peer car-sharing operation.
- **Weeels** (weeels.org): Order cabs and share rides with this smartphone app.
- **Avego** (avego.com): Avego matches drivers and riders in real time as they travel.

Media (Books, Movies, Games, Music)

- **BookMooch** (bookmooch.com): Give away books you no longer need in exchange for books you really want.
- **Swap.com** (market.swap.com): Swap.com allows you to swap what you have for what you need, with an especially good selection of books, movies, music and games.

- **Goozex** (goozex.com): Trade video games and movies.
- **Paperback Swap** (bit.ly/E2Cr): Trade paperback books for free. The same site offers swaps of CDs and DVDs.

Clothing

- **The U.W.A.P. Team** (theswapteam.org), **Clothing Swap** (clothingswap.com), **Swap for Good** (swapforgood.org) and **The Swapaholics** (theswapaholics.com): Check these sites for clothing swaps near you.
- **How to Throw a Community Swap Meet** (bit.ly/bu KOZ2): Find out how to host your own swap.
- **Renttherunway** (renttherunway.com): Rent authentic designer clothing for up to 90 percent off retail prices.
- **Swapstyle.com** (swapstyle.com): At this interactive fashion website, members can swap, rather than buy, unlimited designer clothes with each other.
- **Bag Borrow & Steal** (bit.ly/ccO9ut) and **Fashionhire** (fashionhire.co.uk): Rent designer handbags and accessories at affordable prices.
- **ThredUp** (thredup.com): When the time comes to start a family, use this site to swap children's clothing, toys and books with other parents.

Redistribution Sites (where unneeded stuff finds a loving home)

- **Freecycle** (freecycle.org): This is the original grassroots organization for giving and getting free stuff in your town.
- **craigslist** (craigslist.org): This is the ultimate free classified site with categories for free stuff, barters, sublets, garage sales, house swaps, an incredible selection of used stuff for sale and more. New in town? You can set yourself up with a job, an apartment, furniture and a date all from this site.

- **eBay** (ebay.com): On this international online auction you can buy from and sell to other individuals.

Renting and sharing of general goods where you live

- **Rentalic** (rentalic.com), **Neighborgoods** (neighborgoods.net), **Keepio** (keepio.com) and **SnapGoods** (snapgoods.com): These are the leading peer-to-peer rental and sharing marketplaces.
- **Jointli** (Jointli.com): Do you want to co-own something? This is the perfect tool to buy, use, and manage a shared asset together like cars, tools, real estate, and more.

Campus

- **Chegg** (chegg.com): Rent expensive textbooks on the cheap.
- **Better World Books** (betterworldbooks.com): Save big on used textbooks.
- **CafeScribe** (cafescribe.com): With this new service you can download electronic copies of your textbook, add friends and share your notes.
- **Grade Guru** (gradeguru.com): This is a student class-note sharing site.
- **Free Technology Academy** (bit.ly/fEmIdl): Free college classes on open-source technology and standards.
- **Open Courseware Consortium** (ocwconsortium.org/courses): Find free college courses by scores of top universities from around the world.
- **MITOpenCourseware** (ocw.mit.edu/index.htm): Find free online classes from one of the top technology universities in the world.

If you don't see the sharing solution you need, check out the huge list of how-to-share guides on **Shareable** (shareable .net/how-to-share).

3. Press the power button

Once you discover local opportunities for sharing and collaborating, it's time to hold the power button in. Get involved. Create a profile on a sharing/renting/bartering site and actually list some stuff you could trade. Contact the moderator of a local offline sharing group and offer your goods or services.[18] Collaborative consumption requires a venture into a social world, even if it's only online; you need to get out there.

4. Sync with other devices and enjoy

Ideas like eBay, Netflix and GameFly are pretty well-known examples of sharing, but it's important to remember that options exist offline as well. Sure, the Internet makes it safe for us to share with strangers, but that doesn't mean you should forget about the satisfaction of sharing face-to-face. Coworking brings collaboration into your professional life;[19] a local food co-op brings sharing into your pantry,[20] and skill-sharing communities bring camaraderie to your weekend hobbies.[21]

Don't be afraid to let sharing/bartering/collaborating go viral in other areas of your life as well. You'll discover, as Rachel Botsman does in What's Mine is Yours, that "over time, these experiences create a deep shift in consumer mind-set. Consumption is no longer an asymmetrical activity of endless acquisition but a dynamic push and pull of giving and collaborating in order to get what you want. Along the way, the acts of collaboration and giving become an end in itself."[22]

Stranger Dinners
ARIANNA DAVOLOS

Dear Stranger,

I think we need to talk.

My mom always told me never to talk to you, even if you offered me candy. The news tells me not to trust you—that you will kidnap, rape, rob or kill me, given half the chance.

But I never believed those lies. I know you're just like me, trying to make your world turn as best as you can. I know you have dreams, ideas and favorite recipes just like me. You might even have some insight to share that will make my life better. Maybe you know my future partner. Maybe you know the solution to something I've been trying to figure out for a long while.

Sometimes I run into you at parties, bars and parks. All over, really. I know we just never get a chance to really sit down together. Get intimate. You just always look so busy, and I don't want to intrude. You might think I'm crazy, or hitting on you or something. But I'm not.

Because the thing is, you're really easy to talk to. I can really be myself around you. I can tell you anything, things even my closest friends don't know. I can be really honest.

Technology is changing so fast now. There are so many new ways we can communicate. We can trade books, furniture, stories, sexual partners and ideologies. But it still feels so impersonal. I find myself staring at my computer, isolated, as you walk by my window.

I'm tired of the silent treatment. I hate pretending to ignore you, not knowing when and if to smile when you pass. I don't want to feel afraid when I hear your footsteps behind me at night.

Well, it's time for a change. Come over for dinner. Let's sit down, eat and finally have a chance to really talk. I think this will be a great opportunity for us. In fact, it might save the world, or at least help us work better together. Next week, let's do it at your house.

All my love,

Ari

●●●●●●●●●●●●●●●●●●●●●●●

I don't know why I started the Stranger Dinners. Maybe it was out of loneliness. I was living in a new town with my two best friends, having just graduated from college, where hundreds of familiar and interesting faces would greet me as soon as I walked out my door. I had been so excited to finally be free of the isolated bubble of school. I thought it was holding me back, with its assignments and requirements and obligatory hoops to jump through. I was ready to be set free so I could finally do what I wanted: make art.

I often likened concentrating in sculpture to majoring in possibilities. As I learned more and more about contemporary art practice and theory, my definition of what art was and what it could be expanded until there were no limits. A sculpture could be anything from an idea to an action, a crafted situation, a social experiment, a conspiracy, a business venture, an anecdote told at a party. I spent my last semester trying to walk on the edge of what art could be. I planned field trips, elaborate parties, chance meetings, experiential devices and rumors. I was a little misunderstood but very happy, and I was excited for the day when I would graduate and have the freedom to do even more.

It soon hit me that school hadn't prepared me for the reality that lay beyond. In the real world, people didn't have time to make art. Work that actually earned money took over life. I longed for the creative collaboration between people who had time to philosophize, to create, to experiment, to discuss, to learn and to teach. In school, I had been isolated, but at least I was with hundreds of fellow students and faculty. In the real world, I felt, everyone lived in their own little world, working to pay their rent and provide for themselves.

Working part time in a frame shop, and spending my free time working on projects alone at my house, I felt a very basic, almost laughable, question begin to surface.

What is everyone doing?

I felt as though I had missed something. Is this it? You have a few friends; you wake up, go to work, pay rent and get in some fun when you can? I would make a painting and look at it, thinking, *What is this for?* I wondered how other people were spending their time. How were people figuring out how to balance their obligations with their pleasures? How did they make decisions? How do we all decide what is right for us—what to sacrifice and what to invest? What city to live in? What jobs to apply for? What to do with our lives?

I asked everyone I came across what their life was like. Did they like what they were doing? How did they do it? Why did they like it? How did they get to that point? What did they do before? What were the obstacles? What were the perks? What were the downfalls?

I felt like I was lost in this big labyrinth and the whole world was at a party in the center of it.

Slowly it dawned on me: no one has the answer. There is no right path. Everyone stumbles their way through. Some people get lucky breaks; some people have lower expectations; some people are unhappy; some people are happy. It is always changing and evolving. Everyone just works with what they have, and from their own perspective.

So what if we all started collaborating? What if we shared our perspectives? Not just with our family and friends but with everyone? I wanted to know what a real life was like, and movies weren't really helping.

The Internet has been a huge tool for doing just this. We can share the most intimate details of our lives with strangers, from vacation pictures to opinions, from skin infections to the latest fashions. People type out their greatest fears, aspirations, confessions and successes for the vast unknown sea of people to read and comment on. This gives access to a seemingly infinite amount of information without having to even get out of bed.

But there's something isolating about the Internet. This screen we use as a portal to connect ourselves to each other creates an invisible barrier between ourselves and others. The voyeuristic nature of Facebook allows us to keep up with our acquaintances and friends without their even knowing, without the exchange that let's them know we care and without actually having any kind of substantial relationship with these people.

I just clicked over to someone's Twitter page. I don't know this girl, but I've been following her life for almost a year. The background on her Twitter page says, "I thought I was a narcissist. That is, until I met the rest of the Internet." It's true, we are all broadcasting the stories of our lives. (Some more than others.) We are posturing as ourselves in order to make superficial connections with as many people as possible. Social capital is suffering from inflation. It's not enough to have 50 people in real life you really care about, you have to have 500 Facebook friends too. What? You don't have 1,000 followers on Twitter? You might as well be shouting into the void, because no one hears what you say.

Communication has been one-sided too long. We are starting to learn how to make all this technology work for us. It's starting to occur to people that these amazing networks we are building can help us improve the communities where we actually exist. With the Internet, I can now find all the garage sales in my neighborhood, order takeout, find a date, join a pillow fight and locate my favorite food cart when I get that special craving.

In response to all these ideas and questions, I started inviting strangers to my house for a potluck. With the Stranger Dinners, I seek to bridge the gap between personal and impersonal, between the mass communication and face-to-face interaction. I want to bring what is good about the Internet and relocate it from the ephemeral everywhere and nowhere plane and bring it closer. I want to create the opportunity for people to find something they might not think to look for. I want to take the idea of StumbleUpon.com and bring it to the dinner table. Let us cultivate an open flow of information without the anonymity. That way, the value placed on the information or opportunities we come across is tied to real people who live in our physical communities. I want the humanity back. Instead of going to the library and researching on the Internet, I want to stroll through the stacks, smell the pages of old books, pick a random book off the shelf and let some serendipity into my life.

Most of all, I want to keep myself open to the physical world around me, and all the people who live there. I want us to act as though we have the world in common. If we're all in this together, we'll have all the support we need to get us through. Through my art practice, I seek to create situations outside of our everyday expectations of the world. I strive to actively create what I find lacking from my everyday experience. And I want to explore the possibilities that can come from encouraging people to talk to each other without reason, motivation, agenda, self-selection or presumption. They're no telling what we will find if we just look outside of our everyday experience.

Since I started having Stranger Dinners, they have turned into one of the most fun and easy activities to plan. They are always different, but I've never had one I didn't enjoy. With a little forethought, having a Stranger Dinner can be a great way to meet some new people, gain some different perspectives, and get people to bring delicious food to your house for free.

Think about why you want to have a Stranger Dinner.

Imagine what you'd like to get out of this experience. What is your motivation for the dinner? What makes a night with strangers appealing to you? Write down your intention for the dinner and what you hope to experience. Include this in your invitation, and you will attract people who want the same thing and who are open to letting this experience happen.

How to host your own stranger dinner

Invite strangers

Depending on your comfort level, there are different ways to do this. For the first Stranger Dinners, I found strangers by giving invitations to friends and asking them to invite people they knew. If you go this route, make sure you leave plenty of time for invitation delivery and for people to RSVP. This is probably the safest way to organize a Stranger Dinner, since your friends will have vouched for each guest who attends. If you want to start a dinner series, you can ask the guests to invite the next round of strangers. In this way, the dinner becomes a kind of chain letter.

Another way to invite people is through the Internet. Though I wouldn't necessarily post Stranger Dinner invitations on Craigslist, I do send the invitation to a mailing list or two that I trust, as well as to my own personal contacts. It's easy to find a niche mailing list that speaks to a community you may be comfortable inviting without getting that icky stranger-danger feeling in your stomach. Having said that, posting it on a site like Craigslist might turn up great people, and you may have no problem at all. Follow your gut. Diverse sources of strangers help the dinners stay strange.

Stranger Dinners are best planned on a Sunday or a weeknight. On Fridays and Saturdays people have lots of options and plans that come up at the last minute. Planning on the right day minimizes being stood up by flaky strangers.

Send a reminder

People have a lot of stuff going on. It's easy to forget something you signed up for, especially if it was more than a week ago. A couple of days before the dinner, send your guests a reminder e-mail. Restate the time, day, intentions and location of the dinner, as well as any special instructions. I ask my guests for a question they would like to ask a stranger. These questions serve as confirmation that they have read the e-mail and are still planning to come to the dinner, and they work as great conversation starters to get people talking at the actual dinner.

Prepare your space

It's fun to get excited about the Stranger Dinner. Get your space ready for guests. Make it cozy. Make it easy for people to come in, put down their stuff and relax. Candles, flowers, tablecloth, music—whatever mood you want to set, ambiance is the key!

Make something yummy

I don't like to tell people what to bring for the potluck. I like to be surprised, and I've never been disappointed with the meal. However, I do make sure I have some wine or beer on hand. Alcohol, though not necessary, definitely works as a social lubricant and gets people relaxed and talking.

There is no need to spend all day slaving over a hot stove. Depending on my mood, my budget and my schedule, I make sure my potluck item is stress free and delicious. Stranger Dinners, unlike other dinner parties, are great places to try out new recipes. If it turns out bad, there will be plenty of other things to eat, and you never have to see these people again!

Enjoy!
Now all that's left is to sit back, relax and let a bunch of people bring you food and entertain you for the evening. You're in for a treat! Don't forget to be a courteous host. Make sure everyone feels safe, comfortable, and is never without something to drink. Help people do their final preparations for their dish if they need it and help them serve it up. Don't be afraid to use some ice-breakers if things aren't flowing naturally. People are there to hang out, and after a while you'll be talking like old friends.

When it's time to leave, thank everyone for coming. Make sure they get any leftovers or dishes they brought to take home. If they would like to exchange contact information, send a group e-mail to everyone so they can stay in touch!

Eating Rich, Living Poor

MELISSA WELTER

Tomato Soup

I yellow onion
I tbsp olive oil
2 cans of cannellini beans
6 tomatoes
½ cup of white wine or apple juice
½ tsp each of salt, pepper, and oregano

1. Dice the onion and caramelize with olive oil in a medium frying pan.
2. Cut up the tomatoes and add to the pan. Stir.
3. After about five minutes, pour the wine or juice into the pan.
4. Blend the beans in a food processor.
5. Once the liquid in the pan has reduced by a third, add the beans.
6. Add the spices. Taste. Simmer for another five minutes. Serve.

First, gather your fruits

(Lowest food bill June 2008 to December 2008: $177)

It started disastrously. Three bare months before my partner and I moved, at the start of the worst economic downturn since the Great Depression, I was diagnosed with celiac disease. There was no cure, only a strict diet to be followed. No more gluten, which meant no wheat, rye or barley. Those three ingredients seemed to be in everything. No cookies, no crackers, no soups, no bread, no pasta, no potpies. Nothing.

I couldn't even add soy sauce to my stir fry. It was winter, and the cold was already taking a toll on me. Long, cloudy months lowered my spirits. Winter cut through my jacket and bit at my bones.

It felt like starvation.

Those last months before moving are a blur, a struggle with rice and tepid "tamale" pies, food tasting like ash under the weight of despair. I struggled saying goodbyes to friends, the comfort of a meal out or a potluck at someone's house denied to me. I eked out what I could from a job I hated, trying desperately to balance need against meaning. It was snowing when we left.

The difference between March in Washington and April in California was a season. Spring was in full-throated bloom when we arrived, flowers and bird song permeating my mom's home. Even as we scrambled to find a place to live, being surrounded by family soothed something in me. The sunlight helped. My mother, who also had celiac disease, helped. The shadow of terror that had been sleeping at the edge of my vision faded, melting into hope.

I wish that was the last of it. I wish I learned food again with my mother and then life went smoothly forward. But the spring we moved was the beginning of the economic crash. It took eight increasingly desperate months to find work.

That summer my tomato sprouts died, and we discovered there wasn't a single store in town that had enough gluten-free food for me to survive on. We took long drives to the co-op in San Francisco, stocking up a month's worth of food at a time. I gritted my teeth at liquefying spinach and soft apples, furious as I bent to beg my family for help. I sweated my way through interview after interview as temperatures topped one hundred. Frustration kept my stomach in knots, but still my body healed.

The obsessive heat crushed me. It stole my determined optimism, sucked the heartiness from my spirit. It left me limp sometimes, trying to cover dizziness in interviews for jobs I wasn't qualified for or had no interest in. I made myself fake it, pulling on a mask of perkiness and dropping it w̶h̶e̶n̶ ̶I̶ ̶l̶e̶f̶t̶ ̶t̶h̶e̶ ̶i̶n̶t̶e̶r̶v̶i̶e̶w̶.

Some days I didn't want to get up. Some days I sat at my computer and couldn't make myself look at one more job site or send off another résumé. *Do it,* I told myself, *just do it.* I fought the heat with bottles of water and the depression with a teeth-grinding stubbornness. If I didn't have an interview, I would exercise or meditate or write. I forced myself to do something productive every single day.

I didn't always make it. Some days, I curled up, small and miserable. I gave up. I didn't deny myself those moments; I acknowledged the weight of pain I was carrying. But the next day, I started over again.

Sometimes at the end of a day, all that kept me from crying was a small bowl of ice cream, the taste creamier than anything else I had tried in the years when dairy made me sick. Without gluten, every other food I hadn't been able to eat was suddenly possible again. The first time I ate goat cheese, it smeared over my tongue and left me blissful with its sharpness. After seven years when a single piece of cheese had left me sweating and sick, being able to eat again broke something open in me.

As the heat retreated and the first hints of the coming rain teased at the sky, I found work I loved as a tutor.

Measure out the spices

(Lowest food bill January 2009 to June 2009: $168)
The first Thanksgiving after giving up gluten I was filled with gratitude. Living in the same state as my family meant a shared Thanksgiving dinner for the first time in years. I

had learned, over the past ten months, to dread going out. Potlucks no longer meant pleasure but deprivation. While friends feasted, I was forced to be content with carrot sticks. Even the dip on vegetable trays was a dubious mystery that I was unwilling to risk my health on. "It's fine," I told everyone. "No problem. I like carrot sticks." Sometimes, I even convinced myself. Determination to make this time different pushed me to try my hand at some baking. I didn't want to settle.

My apple pie was a two-part affair: the apples, which smelled perfectly like my childhood, and the crust, which flaked disappointingly. It fell apart as it was served, leaving me chagrined but resolved to do better. The gravy was made in a last-minute hurry as the table was set. I stirred the drained juices from the turkey into butter and rice flour; it thickened deliciously. Around the table, relatives blinked in surprise as they took bites of mashed potatoes and turkey. Across from me, my aunt smiled and pointed out the basket of gluten-free rolls, the turkey, the green beans and salad, my sister's butternut squash soup. Mashed potatoes and garlic mashed potatoes and cranberries and three separate pies that I could eat. I almost cried and felt rich again for the first time in months.

That winter was better.

Remove the tops; chop

(Lowest food bill July 2009 to December 2009: $139)
Buoyed by my success, I learned how to make vegetable stock from scratch. I filled the house with the smells of onion, carrots and bay leaves for long days at a time. I read up on the seasonal plants and grew sugar snap peas and radishes in the small patch I was cultivating in our front yard. That first taste as I picked them off the vine echoed the air around me: crisp and fresh, but unexpectedly sweet.

By the time I pulled the radishes from the ground, I was living less desperately paycheck to paycheck. I poured myself into my work as I did into my garden, tending to struggles with math with the same attention I spent on freeing my geranium from weeds. The care I spent opened a space for something new to grow. My heart filled with young sprouts and the sounds of a child learning to read. I was learning to sustain myself.

Growing food from seed was a magical experience. I tested the air and worried over weather reports before choosing a day. I pressed seeds carefully into the ground, covering them and marking the spot in my mind. Each day, I pressed a finger into the soil to check for dampness, eagerly observing my cultivated patch. Were there sprouts yet? Was that a weed or the first sign of radishes? The leaves, when they came, were green ovals, easily distinguished from the long strings of creeping grass. I watched with happiness lightening my heart as they grew bigger, daring to pull one after two weeks to check the size. I carried my prize inside, washed it in the sink, and ate the radish raw right there in four quick bites. It left me glowing and accomplished.

I taught myself to make bread without wheat or rye, to roast potatoes with onions and vinaigrette, to marinate tofu in spices and sauce. I nibbled cautiously on fresh beets and took peas to potlucks. My heart lifted each time someone bit into food I had made or grown and stopped in delight. Spearmint covered my garden, and I brought handfuls inside and hung them up to dry. For a solid week I took a deep breath every time I came home from work, and then I crumbled the leaves into a jar to keep for loose tea. Fumbling along, I taught myself what foods were in season and tried arugula for the first time. I tossed fingerling potatoes with a little butter and garlic.

Egg and Potato Salad

1½ lbs yellow potatoes, cooked and cubed
3 hard-boiled eggs, chopped
1 small red onion, chopped
¾ cup mayonnaise
2 tbsp spicy mustard
Salt to taste
Combine, cool and serve.

I bought a six pack of tomato seedlings and planted them. I watched them like a hawk, lingering over the soil, checking for dryness or too much dampness. The sprinkler combated the heavy summer sun. I looked at the tomato leaves and rejoiced at the first small yellow flowers. Then green tomatoes began appearing in clumps. It astonished me that six plants could produce so much food. For months, I picked two or three tomatoes every week. I ate them on sandwiches and shared them with friends. I stir-fried them, sautéed them into sauce, froze them, roasted them slowly in the oven.

How to Roast Tomatoes

Preheat the oven to 425.
Cut off the tops and cut the tomatoes in half.
Brush the cut side with olive oil.
Sprinkle with salt or pepper.
Put the tomatoes face down on a cooking sheet and sprinkle on a little more olive oil.
Roast for 25–30 minutes until sweet.

This, I knew instinctively, was food done right.

Simmer together, slowly

(Lowest food bill January 2010 to June 2010: $110)
After that, the gains came in a flurry. I discovered that the

cooperative where I shopped offered a ten percent discount on any food bought as a case. I turned our unused laundry nook into a pantry and moved food in. Chili and rice cakes and refried beans filled the shelves. Even as gas prices spiked, adding transportation costs to food costs, my food bill dropped. I filled half ⟨⟨⟨illegible⟩⟩⟩ and roasted them in the oven. I made apple pie and yam fries sprinkled with parsley fresh from the garden.

I got inspired about local food. Farmers' markets, a staple before I moved, entered my life again. I learned that I could walk to our small town market on Saturdays and get food from two towns over. I discovered that there were U-pick farms for berries and peaches, apples and pears, tomatoes and pumpkins, right where I lived. Buying these foods felt like a gift, like an affirmation that food was life. I began to check the labels to find out where food came from, sticking mostly to food grown nearby. California, warm and geographically diverse, kept me fed locally year round.

Buoyed by my successes, I turned the money I was saving back into my food shopping, the same way I turned compost into the garden and inspiration into the children's lessons. Bulk-food savings became a sturdy cast-iron skillet. Ten percent discounts became a case of mason jars. I tried my hand at making strawberry jam and blueberry cobbler and watched with pleasure as it disappeared off the table at potlucks. I asked for a pressure canner and this year, when the harvest ripens, I will put away spaghetti sauce and green beans and anything else I please.

Eat

(Lowest food bill June 2010 to December 2010: $118)
It is winter again, everything cold around me, but I am content. Poverty didn't starve me; it fed me. Soon, I will go outside and prune my apple trees and hope they bear fruit

for the first time this year. Soon, I will take the pesto made from rich bunches of last summer's basil out of the freezer and add it to corn pasta. Soon, I will open the seed catalogue and plan for radishes and spinach, carrots and tomatoes, dill and thyme. Soon, I will give thanks: for the diagnosis and the poverty that led to my DIY eating adventures. The taste of these years explodes on my tongue.

Flexible Lives, Flexible Relationships
LAUREN WESTERFIELD

Trying to seem as nonchalant and low-mainte-
nance as possible, I declined his offer to use the
single pair of rubber dishwashing gloves that
hung beside the open-air sink. It was evening and
mid-winter; yet the Baja sunset glowed warm as
we took our first stab at partnership over after-
dinner cleanup duty.

In a manner I imagined both ironic and cute, I reversed the
offer.

"I'm good, thanks. Why—did you want to wear them?"

He neither hesitated nor seemed to detect my arch tone.

"Of course I'll take them, if you're sure," he said. "I like to
keep my hands soft."

Still gazing down at the mountain of soiled plates and tumblers piled precariously before me, I laughed at his little joke before looking up. What I saw was a young, recently separated Air Force captain in flip flops and gym shorts, matter-of-factly scrubbing away, bright-pink-rubber-clad fingers illuminated against his deeply tanned and (I suddenly noticed) visibly smooth skin. There was something so sweetly incongruous about his appearance at that moment—meticulous hands at work under a high-and-tight service haircut just beginning to grow free, his dark beard making such earnest domesticity all the more unexpected—that I couldn't help but smile. All my thoughts of a snappy retort vanished. He hadn't been joking; and I, almost exclusively accustomed to smart-ass one-liners and layers of innuendo when it came to conversations with men my age, was instantly disarmed.

Over the course of the next three weeks, I would come to learn that the Air Force captain-turned-yogi hated washing dishes. He infinitely preferred ironing or vacuuming, any of the tidier and more meditative chores (while I had always loved to get my hands dirty). I would discover that he did indeed strive to keep his hands and feet and face soft and healthy—though he'd admit it to other men only if he was asked—and that despite a history of wretched communication skills and gang violence, video games and ministerial aspirations, military service and a mess of perspectives with which I would never have imagined myself able to reconcile, he and I could connect in the deepest and most honest way. We could create the kind of exploded, innovative, vulnerable and yet resilient relationship that I never thought possible until I broke from the pressure-laden bounds of a heavily constructed social grid.

Looking back—shit, even as it was happening—I knew that my experience was atypical. That sun-drenched yoga camp created an extreme version of the broader cultural moment, an unforeseeable crash course in the obliteration of social norms. Neither love nor revolution nor the imminent recession could have been further from my mind when I quit my office job and took off for Mexico, but the fact that they found me there despite the siege of traditional social patterns, might give us a model for millennial-style romance. Something more flexible (if you'll pardon the pun) than the old standards we all know by heart.

That said, living with unstructured love isn't easy. Abandoning the relationship roadmap handed down from our parents' generation may sound liberating, but it comes with a host of uncertainties, a bunch of nagging questions about money and autonomy, biology and gender roles, expectations and stability, and longevity and ego-displacement that are more than enough to drive even the happiest couple all kinds of crazy. But hidden within that crazy is a ripe opportunity to make something new. And thanks to rampant unemployment, requisite shared housing and other necessities of our recession-flavored existence, falling back on old norms is no longer an option. In short? Most of us have no choice but to innovate.

Actually, I take that back. We have two choices: innovate or stagnate.

Fast-forward a year or so from the moment my now-boyfriend first donned those pink dish gloves and flipped my world so wonderfully sideways, and you'll find us leaning precipitously toward the latter. A post-yoga camp interlude of nomadic wandering and seasonal work experiments soon played itself out, and we found ourselves reduced to an increasingly common living situation. That's right—I, along with my expensive liberal arts degree, distressingly patchy résumé, once high-powered boyfriend and our $10 couch, moved back in with my parents.

There was one scenario particular to those homebound days that I especially came to loathe. Whenever my mother's friends or our neighbors popped up at my side in the grocery store (always as I was sifting through produce, hair unkempt, in sweatpants on a Tuesday afternoon) I'd groan inwardly and get ready for the barrage.

"What are you doing these days?" they'd always ask, all smiles, expecting to be impressed.

Did they not notice the sweatpants? The glasses? The grocery shopping in our wee tiny town on a weekday? All signs pointed to unemployment.

"Oh, I'm staying with my family right now," I'd say calmly, feigning confidence and an implied visit rather than permanent residence. "I'm between things and taking a break to help mom out around the house."

"Between what kind of things?" My interlocutor would inevitably press me, hungry for gossipy details.

"Well, I'm sort of writing… " I'd say, trailing off. "Actually, my boyfriend and I are looking at maybe teaching English overseas." A vague truth surfaces, providing distraction, giving me something to say, no matter how irrelevant, that might satisfy.

"How exciting! And are you two planning on getting married?"

"No no, not yet," I'd say, forcing a smile while suppressing exaggerated eye rolls and a variety of panicked expletives.

"So you're just…living at your parents' house? Together? And not really doing much of anything?"

Most folks were too polite to draw this conclusion out loud; but I always heard it anyway, their judgment ringing clear over supermarket jingles and wailing, unruly children as if pronounced through a bullhorn. Because this exchange, no matter how well-meaning or innocently intentioned, was a booby trap, a sociocultural snare the likes of which entangle any of us who fail to conform to the supposed status quo. It's nonsense—and yet a notion so deeply ingrained as to confuse even the most sure-footed 20-something seeking an authentic way in the world.

Pinned on the edge of a produce bin, under pressure to say something acceptable, I always found it difficult to tell the straight truth: we were not aimless degenerates, only stuck in an extended state of flux. We knew, after countless hours of raw and honest conversation, that we needed time to figure out the most sustainable way in which to nurture our relationship and respective goals while still making enough cash to fly the coop. We weren't alone in this dilemma, and yet somehow it always sounded strange when I said it out loud.

Perhaps this is because, as times have changed, so too has youthful non-conformity. Not everyone feels the need to disappoint their parents on purpose; and some of us, grateful for the comfort they've provided, still hope to impress. Yet the very notion of success today is under construction. Many of us have observed the grown-ups, detected their patterns and watched them fail. If our lives don't fit their mold anymore, we've got to break it; but how do we tell them that? And where the hell are we to start?

For us, the answer came crashing down in the form of my parent's divorce. In light of the strained domestic situation, what began as a string of sitcom-worthy inconveniences soon became a perilous onslaught. We found ourselves in the crosshairs of a dissolving marriage, and took shelter from the emotional shrapnel by vowing never to repeat their mistakes. It was a silver lining of the strangest variety: without that unforeseen return to the parental nest, we might never have realized how necessary it was to do something different, something more fluid and malleable to suit hearts fated for change.

By this stage in life, someone—mother, father or high school counselor—has usually urged us to put career at the forefront, to never let a sweetheart tie us down. But what if today's economy, job market and social culture have mutated and conspired to change all that, to encourage us to put partnership first? With cash growing scarce and jobs even scarcer, human connection is the biggest asset we have. Knocked swiftly off the adult hierarchy, we suddenly have the chance to find inspiration in the most unexpected people, places and ideas.

This is probably for the best. Because frankly, the old maps just don't work anymore when it comes to charting a 20-something's way in the world. This doesn't mean plenty of us won't at some point find steady work, get married, have kids or purchase the greenwashed version of a minivan, but it does mean that most of us will do it in our own way, maybe skipping some steps or performing them in an unorthodox fashion. These behaviors are sure to dismay sweet old aunties and grannies who want only to find us the ephemerally defined "good husbands," "great jobs" and "perfect weddings" of days gone by.

Take me, for instance. Now, at 26, after three years of pitifully part time or completely unpaid employment, I've finally landed a "real" job writing copy for a social media marketing company. Ironic, right? That my first adult paycheck is completely dependent on a purely millennial innovation many grown-ups are still tacitly afraid of? I don't think it's a coincidence. On the contrary, I consider it the sharpest evidence of our altered world—one in which, more than ever, communication is key. My boyfriend and I are still learning how to navigate this world, living as free of old constructs as possible, and sometimes finding it utterly strange. I'm reminded of this every day as I get up, get dressed, brush my hair like a real grown-up and go to work while my boyfriend sits, reads, contemplates and otherwise absorbs the universe as he searches for his niche in our new life. (I should note that he also does the laundry and vacuuming, which is delightful, while I pull my weight on weekends, wash the dishes and wear pink gloves now, every time.)

Maybe we'll get married one day; maybe we won't. Great things may lie ahead for us—and then again, perhaps we'll opt for scraping by and simple pleasures, a life with lots of time for cheap wine and sandy feet and purring cats. I'll be the first to admit that I don't know where we're headed, that unemployment put our relationship to the test more than once and made us grow up faster than we may have liked. But with communication on our side, somehow, everything seems possible. And the wider the net we cast, the more friends and couples we find to connect and share ideas with over box wine on our $10 couch, the stronger our optimism grows. I like to think of us as floating rather than climbing, hands clasped and stretching outward to receive the future as it comes.

Who Needs an Ivory Tower?

JENNA BRAGER

SHARE or DIE

SHARE or DIE

Detroit, Community Resilience and the American Dream
MILICENT JOHNSON

When I told my friends and family I would be traveling to Detroit to write about community resilience, I got the same reaction from everyone: silence. Then, slowly, as if not to offend me, people would look at me very seriously and say, "Be very careful—you never hear anything good about Detroit. Remember, you're a woman—you have more to lose from an attack than just your wallet." Frequently the conversation would trail to the murder rate or economic devastation and point out that "desperate times make people do crazy things." My surprise at this reaction was compounded by the fact that those words weren't coming just from my parents; they were coming from born-and-bred city folks who know that the greatest cities always get a bad rap from people who have never been there.

This series of odd reactions made me more determined to go see the city for myself. I had a sneaking suspicion that Detroit was just like my beloved New York City: gritty, homey and real in all the right places, with a community spirit missed by those just passing through.

But the voices of my friends and family warning me of the potential of physical harm did get to me. I have an embarrassing confession to make: despite being a New York City kid who has little fear of traveling alone, I bought pepper spray. If anything dangerous really did happen, I would probably clumsily spray myself in the face, so I knew that it was more about silencing the voices of concerned family and friends than about actual protection.

So, with my pepper spray and intuition in tow, I took a trip to see what the all fuss was about.

I wasn't sure what to expect when I got off the plane and left the airport. Would I walk out to a Spartan city that, as pictures of Detroit would lead one to believe, looked like a war zone?

The moment I got into a cab I knew everything was going to be fine. I was delighted to find that, just like in every great city, everything you could possibly want to know can be learned from a cab driver. My cab driver, who had moved to Detroit from Yemen some ten years earlier, told me that, while Detroit can be a dangerous place full of racial tensions, it has become home because of the friends he's met here and the community that has welcomed him.

After a few minutes of typical highway driving, we arrived at the Inn on Ferry Street, a collection of Victorian houses preserved by the historical society. The entire block was a magical collection of houses that took me back to a time in which barons would build 17-bedroom houses just because they could. It was a preserved snapshot of the regality of the US in its heyday.

While fidgeting with my key, I met a woman named Rachel Lutz, and my magical journey began. She asked me what I was doing in town. I said, with some apprehension, "Writing about community resilience." She responded, "Well you'll have to meet all of my friends." Within 15 minutes I had the numbers of young entrepreneurs and people starting their own nonprofits, as well as established nonprofit and foundation types.

When I expressed how overwhelming I found her kind gesture to a complete stranger, she said, "It's my pleasure. So many people come here for 'devastation porn.' They come here to look at the abandoned buildings and devastation, but there's something even greater here that people should be paying attention to. Right now, Detroit, and particularly this neighborhood, Midtown, is where the rebirth is being fostered by 20-somethings who are quitting their jobs, cashing in their savings or pulling together a little capital, and going for their dreams. This is one of the few places left where, if you are willing to put up a little capital, you can make your dream, whatever it is, come true. We live in the biggest small town you'll ever experience, and everyone's ready to pick up a shovel and work with you to build the future."

I couldn't agree more. And for the record, I threw out my pepper spray the very next day.

So, what does this have to do with community resilience? Let me tell you.

Detroit, in a lot of ways, parallels the track we are on as a nation. After an industrial boom in the late 19th century, Detroit became a hub of commerce and a place where people could come to find opportunity. At the beginning of the 20th century Detroit became synonymous with the automobile industry. As the industry branched out to become an influence in city planning around car dependency, suburbanization and sprawl became a way of life. Suburban isolation and dependence on industry are legacies we tend not to talk about in this country, but as the economy collapses they become hard to ignore. Unresolved racial tensions and the abandonment of cities are facts of life here in the States. Let's be clear, Detroit is not alone in this. It may be more pronounced here, but if we stay on the current track of trying to house ourselves in single-family homes, consuming without regard for practicality or sustainability and looking to a single source for our well-being—in our case, straight-up consumer-driven capitalism—there is no need to look into a crystal ball: the snapshot of our future is staring us in the face in the stereotypical shot's of Detroit.

But I believe Detroit also holds the key to the future of this great nation. We must evolve to a more sustainable way of living if we are to survive, and I think we all innately sense it. We know that two-income-dependent housing prices do not add up while unemployment and underemployment approach the double digits. We know that a growing world population is not going to be able to support a group of people that consumes three times as many resources as the rest of the world. Within our lifetimes, many of us will have to find new ways to meet our needs and will pioneer a new meaning of what "the good life" really is. Those who have stayed in Detroit are pioneers. It's like what happens to a forest after a great fire. At first glance, it looks like everything is dead. But, if you look closer you'll find that the rich soil is fertile and ready for planting. Detroit's ground is fertile and being seeded as you read this.

During my time there, I met with people in their twenties and thirties who had bought storefronts, started art collectives, founded their own nonprofits and, frankly, were living the dream—from the delicious Good Girls Go To Paris Crepes, whose crepes are so good I wake up every morning craving them, to Rachel's Place, a vintage store in Corktown

Credit: Milicent Johnson

that fills an entire house, owned by Rachel Leggs.

The whole city is filled with locally grown, frequently organic, or locally made things to eat, see and enjoy. And the best part is that everyone is really into supporting these businesses. There is a dual pride that comes from supporting your friends and neighbors and also supporting the people who, like you, want to see Detroit thrive. The local pride is as palpable as it is at a Red Sox game, but it lasts much longer than a season. It made everything taste better, worth the price, and it left me with a joy that box stores like H&M or Barnes & Noble never do. All the products I bought and the food I ate were true quality, priced reasonably, made locally and super cute! Imagine that.

Every business owner I talked to echoed the sentiment that their dream of owning a business could not have been fulfilled as successfully as it had been here in Detroit. One of my favorite stops during my week was to the Spiral Collective (a neighbor of Avalon Bakery). Co-owners Janet Jones, Dell Pryor and Sharon Pryor (Dell's daughter) have a shop that has gifts and house treats, a book store and an art gallery. The building was once a barn in the formerly notorious Cass Corridor. Dell reworked it into a comfortable, warm and beautiful space. I popped in to get out of the rain and was immediately greeted, warmed and embraced by these sweet fabulous ladies.

Mother and daughter Dell and Sharon Pryor with long-time friend and co-owner Janet Jones

Not only did I get local art, gifts and books at great prices, they also spoke with me about their experiences as women business owners and artists in Detroit. I got a wonderful dose of history, culture and mentoring every time I went in. It felt oddly like home. This is the shopping experience I've never known I always wanted.

Projects that are changing Detroit: Giving young people a voice in defining their city

Later in the week I met with Mike Han—community development director of "I Am Young Detroit."[23] I met Mike at an event examining the soul of the Detroit community. While stealing a couple of the gratis muffins for lunch, I overheard him explain that a city-wide conversation on Detroit's young people, their potential and what the city has to offer them was necessary.

"I Am Young Detroit" is an effort to dispel the myths about Detroit and highlight the cool, progressive, creative work being done by the under-40 set in the city. It not only highlights events, news and culture of the city, it also puts the spotlight on the emerging creative class—artists, designers, musicians and entrepreneurs who are hustling to great success in the city.

Mike is a young entrepreneur himself, with his blog and brand called Street Culture Mash (SCM), which is a lifestyle brand that is meant to complement a more sustainable and creative lifestyle. SCM offers sustainable art in tangible goods with everything from organic apparel to furniture and fixed-gear bikes. I had already drunk the "I love Detroit" Kool-Aid by the time I got to sit down with him, but talking about the challenges and potential of this great city was like getting an IV of love for this city that is refillable any time I visit either of his sites. Mainly we spoke about what a great city Detroit is for young folks, artists and creative types, and the spirit of helping each other. "Basically, people are excited if you're excited in Detroit. If you want to do something good, people are like, 'I can help with that' or 'Do you know so and so?' Because we're like a small town, people are well connected and willing to use those connections to help you pursue your dream."

We also talked about city government. The city has been rocked with a history of political corruption, and there are very real suburban vs. urban issues that have their roots in racial tensions. The city's 8 Mile Road continues to be the physical barrier between the largely African American city and mostly white suburbs. White flight, which contributed to the city's loss of jobs and tax revenue, and the well-documented discrimination that kept blacks from moving into the suburbs has lead to resentment on both sides with regard to planned revitalization of the city. On the one hand, the city and the suburbs need each other. They need the ideas, people power and investment of industries that moved their operations to the suburbs. On the other hand, it makes sense that some Detroit residents find it insulting that suburban people who have chosen to abandon the city, send their kids to private schools and live in communities protected by police forces would want to have a hand in deciding what the future of the city should be.

There is also a palpable fear in Detroit that once revitalization does happen, gentrification will follow, and once again those who rebuilt the city will have to leave once white, upper class people deem it a posh place to live. As someone who has worked in community development, I hesitated to share this story because I worry that Detroit will become synonymous with places like San Francisco or Williamsburg—places in which "redevelopment" and "revitalization" really means pushing out low- to moderate-income people and people of color. But my hope is that there are enough

Detroit citizens committed to the re-envisioning process early on who will fight with the same fervor they have for years to keep the city theirs. With the introduction of Mayor Bing (who has both supporters and opponents, naturally) and the "Detroit Works Project," which has invited citizens to actively be involved in the city's re-envisioning process, civic engagement, while heated, is also clearly a priority. Almost 1,000 people turned out for the first public meeting to discuss strategies from the consolidation of neighborhoods to the possibility of more public transportation in this historically car-driven city. As Mike said, "We may have a shortage of some things, but one thing there isn't a shortage of is passion for this city."

Putting community development in the hands of the community

Later that night some new friends invited me to Soup at Spaulding, a creative funding initiative started by local community members in North Corktown.[24] The community meets every Thursday to eat a simple, delicious meal of soup (made with ingredients from the community garden Spirit Farm and donations from Avalon Bakery), buy local produce (fresh eggs, jams and beautiful produce) and learn about two community projects that need funding. The $5 admission covers the cost of the meal and goes to whatever project the group votes on. The projects then go up on Kickstarter to get more funding. That night, a woman named Danielle "Doxie" Kaltz, who started the Detroit chapter of a service arm of Burning Man called Burners Without Borders, gave a presentation about a project she created after seeing homeless folks living under bridges. She has been packing backpacks full of blankets, toiletries, food and anything else people might need, and driving around and giving them out to people who are homeless.[25] She won the pot that night.

The room was electrified with the brave and humble efforts of Doxie, who simply saw a need and decided to have the audacity to fill it. But hey, clearly, that's the Detroit way.

Building healthier, more connected, community, one seed at a time

On one of my last days in the city I met Mark Covington, founder of the Georgia Street Community Collective,[26] who, after being laid off from as an environmental engineer and moving back into his family's home, noticed that people were dumping garbage in the empty lots across from his house.

"I knew no one else was going to clean those lots, so I decided I would," he said with a shrug, as if it were simply the logical thing to do. After cleaning the lots only to have them dumped on again, he decided to plant a garden to prevent more dumping. Not only did it work, but community members began to come out of their houses to see what he was up to. Neighborhood kids began to help with the planting and became interested in gardening. People who sensed a connectedness with Mark began to share their difficulties with affording food while paying for heating and electricity.

Mark Covington and Rachel Lutz—at one of the plots that has a playground and greenhouse.

This spurred Mark to begin to grow more and involve the community. In time he developed an outdoor movie night, a "read to your kids" night and community celebration nights.

He bought the building next to his grandmother's house for next to nothing, and he and his brother are doing all the renovations. They hope to have a space to hold more community dinners and celebrations, a computer lab for the kids, a clothing and food donation drop-off space and an emergency fund for community members experiencing tough times. The whole collective now consists of five lots on Georgia Street, including a fruit orchard. Talk about community resilience. Detroit is the embodiment of the DIY movement.

Giving students a chance to design the future

The institutions of Detroit—the College for Creative Studies (CCS) and Wayne State University—as well as both community and global foundations are taking notice and picking up a shovel as well. Amazing strides are taking place with university/foundation partnerships that are funding business incubators, light-rail development projects, partnership development and grants that allow entrepreneurs, researchers, scientists, tech industry folks and artists to live in the city while connecting them to communities in need. The College for Creative Studies has even sent its students out into Detroit to think creatively about how art and design can foster community development. One project in particular, CCS student Veronika Scott's "Element Survival Coat," has garnered national attention. After spending time in homeless shelters, Veronika designed a stylish coat (water proof, self heated and lined with house insulation) that can be turned into a sleeping bag at night. It can be sewn by someone with no prior experience and will hopefully be given at no cost to those who need it. The hope is to empower people who are homeless by employing them to sew the coats and providing them with free housing and meals in addition to a paid job.[27]

"I really think it's a blessing that we've been deconstructed," said Mike. "We just have to build it right this time. If we do, we can show the world how to live in a sustainable way, with a city that can move quickly to adapt to whatever changes comes its way." I couldn't agree more.

So, here's my final confession: I want to move to Detroit. Having lived in New York City, DC, Boston and now San Francisco, I'm used to comfortable city life that caters to the young. But never have I experienced a place thriving with talent, energy, passion and determination to make their city, and by association, the world, a better place. If you are looking for a place to develop your dream, whatever it may be, consider trying to do so in Detroit, in the place I am now dubbing the birthplace of our collective new American destiny. See you there.

Every Guest A Host
Inside a Nomad Base
ROBIN

The doorbell rings. "Password please," crackles over the intercom from inside. "Helicopter," they answer outside.

Real passwords don't belong to this place; the game is just another way to check whether the person is actually coming for this house, and to see how the new visitor might respond. If people say they don't know the password, they are asked to make one up. "But how do you track people?" someone asked once.

We don't.

Welcome to Casa Robino, or simply "Casa" as most people call it, a small apartment in a central neighborhood of Amsterdam that has hosted more than a thousand people over the past three years. They came to "be a host" and share

Credit: John Thackwray[28]

the place, to join in for the weekly vegan open dinner or for some tea. A map of the world on the wall is filled with pins that people leave to mark their places of birth.

As long as I've rented this apartment, I've shared it with people who are lifestyle travelers—nomads. When I began, I described it as a hospitality house, then a shared travelers' home and later as a (perhaps edgier) nomad base. The house is a shared space in the truest sense: visitors are encouraged to see it as their shared place, and hence to care for it as if it were not just their own but one that belongs to everyone present, as well as to the people yet to come.

They make it a better place by offering small acts of kindness, by receiving and giving hospitality. They choose to be part of the growing community of people who have visited already and experienced the type of sharing and hospitality the house offers. Visitors come and contribute what they have and who they are, the space changing with every opening of the door.

But not everyone who comes has to give; some just come to receive. Maybe they need a place to sleep, are tired from a trip or just need to be taken care of—for at least a little while. The group cares for as many people as it can, and things come together best when nobody tries to enforce an arbitrary reciprocity. Every visitor brings a new presence, something it's impossible to measure on any chore wheel.

Tonight the living room is full with people from many places, chattering away. Some are local; others have come from the United States, England, Finland, Argentina and France. Many are travelers, some experienced hitchhikers, sailors or cyclists, and others are people of the first generation of digital nomads, all sharing in some degree a desire for togetherness and an uncharted life.

They celebrate that one of the long-stayers, a young woman from Canada, is parting to continue on a trip that has been her life for five years now, traveling from Australia to here, working in a few countries as a chef, fruit-picker or waitress. Now she's going further to as-yet undetermined places.

The person who rang the doorbell comes in; we share hugs and pass around glasses of wine. The smell from the kitchen, where others prepare food is great, the atmosphere even better.

The house is small, but shared space always expands. "Where can I sleep tonight?" a returning friend asks, and someone answers, "I have some space in the room I'm using." People adapt to the space they are in, and the house is made for adapting.

An example is the living room, called "The Zula." Two couches, one low to the ground and the other a bit higher, a chair in a corner, a mattress and some pillows fill up the sides of the room. In the middle sits a low, round table that seemingly appears out of nowhere when food is ready.

People bring in the pots, pans, plates and cutlery and move around to wedge everyone in. If someone arrives late for dinner, everyone moves a bit closer together.

The cooks introduce the food, where it came from (dumpsters), who fetched it and how it was prepared. Plates are passed around, and different people add food from the pans. Amazingly, no one starts before the food is passed and all are served.

Dinner serving doesn't always go this smoothly, but somehow it works out like this most of the time, even though (or maybe because) there are no fixed protocols or practices. With walls full of unusual art, a bathroom door with brainstorm papers on sharing and randomly left notes and postcards in the kitchen, the space breathes community and lends itself to giving. It's a place for passing plates, for offering food to others before starting to eat yourself.

"Think of others, before you think of yourself" is one of the guidelines of the house. It complements "Share what you want, take what you need" and "As a guest, be a host."

The latter is the most groundbreaking aspect of the house and the major reason why people love it so much and want to set up similar spaces. Here, every guest is both captain and sailor. Both consumer and producer. Tutor and pupil. Not one role or the other, but equal and together. Everyone is the host of everyone.

For the traveler who goes from host to host, from house to farm or from community to the road, life is lived almost always as a guest. Hosts tend to expect the traveler to perform or to entertain them, to listen or tell stories.

For people who live like this, after traveling for years and years, or even for only a couple of months, it is a wonderful thing to finally feel you are home and share with people who live like a family of friends. They get to enjoy the freedom to go further, to stay as long as necessary and, if it fits, to return when they want.

Credit: Robin

When these new hosts arrive, I encourage them to take what we might consider "ownership," but not to own. A room doesn't belong to one person; neither does the bread belong to any individual. Everything is shared, except the things people don't want to share—obvious enough in practice, but sometimes hard to make known and understood.

It's a shocking change for some; most people are not used to giving for the sake of giving. For example, some folks are accustomed to having other people working for them, especially those who just left the traditional family structure. But for the ones who have been traveling for quite some time, it can equally be a challenge to think of everybody's food needs, instead of having to secure their own first, or to clean everyone's dishes and not just their own.

And things do not always work out so fantastically. The bike-sharing project is mostly non-operational, and sometimes people would rather chill and hang out than make things happen. Being in Amsterdam, where people often come to get legally stoned, doesn't always help in that respect either.

But all goes mostly very well; I've found it's the attitude that matters. The bigger problem is often how you deal with things, not the dishes that haven't been done. It is the frustration that costs you energy, not the cleaning. It helps if people understand that if they don't feel they're enjoying doing something in particular, it may be better to leave it for the person who will, and move on to something else.

It is equally important to make people understand how the house functions so well. The things needed (material and immaterial alike) to make the house what it is come from people. You are able to ride this bike because someone who came before you worked his or her butt off. You can eat because someone has cooked and another has cleaned or collected the food. And you can be here free of charge, because someone else does pay the rent, and because people before you left donations to support this way of life.

It is these acts of giving that make "Casa" happen, which is also the essential understanding for community, of how to do this all together. If you want to be parasitic—to put it bluntly—another will have to work harder to make that possible. It's not about what you think other people owe you, but what you receive back from the continuous cycle of giving. The earth is just a nest of ants on a big scale; this house just one planet, so to speak.

The house teaches more lessons: If you want to stay longer, others may not be able to come. If you take this book, you decide it serves you better than the person who comes after you. It's great to have ideals, but being practical and flexible is what allows you to put them into practice.

And of course there are little secrets that make this life work, and mistakes that can make it collapse. If one person or a couple of people take on too big a burden, you know they will eventually fall down—no matter how much love and dedication they put in.

A cycle of people is essential to keeping the house going. The turnover of people avoids entrenching problems in people's relationships with each other, and it keeps the place dynamic. Therefore not all people can stay for long, but hopefully at least long enough to understand the culture of being a host while being guested, and to make sure that they pass this culture on to the next arrival, and maybe even further into their lives.

An important question is how to filter people, in other words, who to accept. Hospitality exchange networks such as Bewelcome[29] and Couchsurfing[30] can help to get the right people in, but the number of requests can easily flood the space's capacity. So instead of relying on these systems, we now have our own website,[31] thanks to one visitor who built it.

First it was just for fun, but later we started using the site to handle the requests, to keep parts of the community together and to be our online presence. As a result, this web-site has become a meta-community to testify people about their stories and it enables them to meet up with other "casa people."

Regardless of the technology, nothing works better than word of mouth and people sending more of the "right people"—the independent traveler who doesn't need much explanation of how these communities function and who loves to meet similar people.

In terms of diversity, the house needs more than nomads; it also needs the student who is just on vacation, the person who works in an office, the activist who fights for social justice, the tech-nomad who loves to hack, the artist who travels as a way of life as well as the traveler who has just left home for the first time. It's in this type of environment that we can make and find mutual inspiration.

I've also learned that you can't ignore stress and feeling burned out. It happens. At times there is simply too much on someone's back and she or he lacks the space to express emotions. Dealing with this can take time. Another kind of sharing may be to get out of somebody's way or to allow some private space.

But the real key to avoiding burnout, the kind of depression that can corrode the foundation of any collective venture, is the mutual care and friendship that provide a sustainable basis. A community is not simply the sum of its people; it is the connection among us all, the intimacy, the love and the space to express our individuality that serves as fuel for our capability and willingness to share with each other.

The night has come to an end. Dinner has been served; we've taken turns toasting our departing friend; we play musical instruments; and others are eating desert. When the last visitor leaves, people go to sleep, and the house comes to rest. I play a bit with the cat, walk around and listen to the (uncommon) emptiness and silence of the place.

This time no one did the dishes, and they're still lying dirty in the sink. I leave them be, to discover the next day that they have vanished. "Why did you do the dishes?" I ask the guy who cleaned the kitchen in the morning, even though he was too tired to join the dinner. "Because they were here," he says.

Screening for Gold
How to Find and Keep your Good Housemate
ANNAMARIE PLUHAR

Mary was scared. Her elation at getting the job she wanted was dampened by her worry about finding a place to live. She knew exactly one person in the city where she would be moving, and her salary wasn't going to be enough to rent an apartment alone. She had to find a housemate, a prospect that seemed daunting and frightening. She would be living with a stranger.

Not everyone feels as uneasy as Mary at the idea of looking for a housemate. Some simply choose a new living situation based on the available room, location, rent and a good gut feeling about their future roomie. They do start out living with a stranger, but it rarely ends that way.

You don't have to move in with a stranger. Ever. While you may start the process looking for a person you don't yet know, by the time he or she moves in, the new housemate should be a known entity, someone suited to you, no longer a stranger. You are looking for your good housemate. Not just someone who also needs a place to live or has a room to spare. While complete unknowns might be okay for stopgap or temporary arrangements, you should select your housemate according to criteria you have established.

A good housemate is someone with whom you can live comfortably. You smile at each other, you chat, you engage and disengage freely with no tension. You have minimal tension because before you consented to live together you discussed how you want to share housing. You made agreements about how you would live together, and you are living up to them. This is key—you make these agreements before you move in.

The evolution from stranger to potential housemate should be a careful process. Each step in the process filters potential partners, weeding out those who are not a good fit until you're left with someone who suits you. Your first step is getting clear on what (and whom) you're looking for.

Most people pay attention to the physical aspects of a new home, such as closets, light, Internet availability, public transportation, bathrooms. In addition to thinking about the space you must also think about how you want to live day to day. Make a list of what you can't live without and what you can't live with. Whether you don't want a television or never turn off ESPN, be self-aware about it. This is a personal inventory of your non-negotiable requirements. It's a good idea to write it down. You may think you already know what these are, but there is something helpful about seeing it in black and white. You can use this worksheet. This is your first step in the screening process.

Once you have a list of essential requirements, you can start looking. In your first contact, most likely by e-mail, find out if your applicant meets your requirements. If not, cut 'em loose. If the prospect looks promising, have a telephone interview. By telephone you get a better feel for the person. If it doesn't seem right, don't continue. If you like what you're hearing, agree to meet in the home.

Meeting in person is the third screening step. Now you talk about the nuts and bolts of sharing housing. This should be a wide-ranging conversation in which you discuss money, kitchen use, cleanliness, neatness, noise, routines and guests. You ask every question that occurs to you. You answer the other person's questions about you and the house honestly. As you talk, you build agreements about how you would live together. Listen to your instincts and hunches. If it doesn't feel right, walk away. If it does, you may have met your new housemate. But you have one more screen: references.

Talk to references. Most likely, the references will validate your feelings. As you do this step, you have time to consider the interview and the agreements made. If all is well, you have found your good housemate.

This process may not feel as linear as it's presented here. There will be disappointments and narrow escapes. But stick to your guns and expect that there is a good housemate also looking for you. When you need someone to help you move a bureau or to just leave you alone once in a while, the effort of finding the right person will all have been worth it.

But your work isn't done yet! Your good housemate is a treasure, and the care that you took in finding her or him cost you time and energy. You want the relationship to work, to be comfortable and easy, mutually beneficial and unstressed. A key to this is to live up to the agreements you made about how you would live when you moved in together. What follows are the most common sticking points for housemates and some harmonious practices worth following.

Money

You pay all bills on time and hold up your end of the financial responsibilities as promised. There are no surprises here.

Kitchen Use

You keep your food items separate, combine them or share certain supplies as was agreed on as part of the interview process. If your food is separate, do not eat or drink what is not yours. Nothing can be more irritating to a housemate than to find something gone. If you share food, make sure one person isn't doing all the cooking or shopping. Make sure housemates are reimbursed for collective purchases in a timely fashion. Clean up after you cook so that the next person doesn't have to deal with your mess.

Cleanliness

People have different ideas of what clean is and whose responsibility it is to do the cleaning. In your interview you agreed on the basics; now you must follow through. There should be a system whereby all housemates know how cleaning happens and can make a note of when they have done their bit. Some households have a chore wheel, others a chart. Some have permanently assigned tasks, while others rotate the tasks. Sometimes a home owner does all the cleaning of common rooms. Whatever your situation, do your bit cheerfully and on time.

Neatness

Though you talked about neatness during the interview, this usually requires some fine-tuning. How much stuff left lying around in common rooms is acceptable? In general, the other person's stuff will seem messier than your own, but he or she may feel the same about your stuff.

Noise

Television, radio, video games, Internet videos and music are all sources of sound in a home. Housemates don't have to like the same sounds to live well together, but they do need to agree on what sounds they are willing to hear in common spaces and at what times. Someone who loves to blast hip-hop music while cooking probably shouldn't live with someone who requires silence. A night owl with a love

·for death metal should probably invest in some headphones. As you live together you may discover new ways that sound is both good and annoying. Talk about it often.

Routines

You need your housemate have a set of expectations about the daily routines. Though it is not so much a negotiated agreement, you agreed to live together in part because your daily routines were complementary. Maybe your housemate has a regular job and is out of the house all day, or is always home for dinner, or leaves every weekend to see a significant other. But life happens and routines can change. A new job, a break-up or a close friend moving in next door will affect how you or your housemate uses the home. Sometimes the transition happens without any tension, but sometimes the new patterns of home use are significantly different and housemates become unsettled and upset.

To keep your good housemate, discuss these changes and how they affect the household. Create a new agreement to make sure that the new routines are satisfactory and comfortable for all.

Guests

Some homes have friends who drop in all the time. Other homes never have visitors. You should have a basic understanding about visitors as part of the agreement you created. Since guests who visit from afar and stay overnight disturb routines, it is essential that your housemates know in advance about the guests. Whether you need to ask permission or simply inform depends on your agreement.

A new lover who starts living in the house can be a major source of irritation; after four days you need to have a conversation about it (and it might be worth consulting the noise section above).

Agreements, not rules

Be true to the agreements you made before you moved in together. Many stories of housemate problems stem from a perceived or actual transgression of spoken and/or unspoken agreements, whether these have to do with completing chores, paying bills or sharing food. Talk to your housemates—and do it in person, not by text or e-mail. Text and e-mail can make a small issue much bigger through misunderstandings endemic to the media.

An agreement is not a rule and should not become one. Rules have hard edges, while agreements have soft edges. Adaptability and flexibility might be called for if an agreement needs to be changed due to changing circumstances. If so, do it consciously and in a spirit of cooperation and generosity. You want your home to be comfortable.

Your agreements are as good as gold. Guard them well.

How to Build
A Housing Co-Op
MIRA LUNA

For a year in college, I lived at a 32-member student housing cooperative where I had more fun than I did in the rest of my time at college combined and met lifelong friends. Because the co-op was owned by a nonprofit (consequently rent would get cheaper relative to inflation), I saved money by living there, so I didn't need to work my way through school. The activists, artists and thinkers who lived there brewed new ideas that planted seeds in me that sprouted years later. We seized the opportunity to use common spaces for political and arts events that we would have never been able to host as regular tenants elsewhere. The house created a vessel for whatever passion we wanted to manifest.

On the downside, I found it incredibly difficult to study there. The work of being a contributing co-op member was a drain on my work time, and there was too much drama to focus on school. The co-op had structure and rules but little follow through, which meant that chores and maintenance didn't get done and conflict was common. We had an application process but let everyone in regardless of their ability to cooperate, as well as people with drug and mental health problems who needed more support than we could offer. New members weren't trained in consensus decision-making, which created heated and way-too-long meetings over trivial issues. I learned a lot about what not to do.

Years later, volunteering for a nonprofit that develops cooperative housing, I discovered that when done properly, resident-owned co-ops can offer an affordable and more convivial alternative to single-family housing. Co-ops save money by cutting out landlords' profits, sharing common spaces, lowering operating costs and receiving public subsidies for affordable housing. Studies show that co-ops provide other benefits, such as greater social cohesion and support, reduced crime, increased civic engagement and sustainability, better quality and maintenance of housing, and resident stability.

Housing cooperatives are defined primarily by their legal structure: co-op members own the housing collectively through shares in an organization, rather than individually, as with condos. Residents also govern the housing democratically, either directly or through elected representatives. Not just for students, co-ops can be home to support groups of low-income families, artists, elderly, disabled and people with a common purpose. Over 1.5 million homes in the US are part of a cooperative housing organization.

There are several kinds of co-ops:

- Rental or leasehold co-ops are democratically run organizations of tenants who equitably share costs of renting or leasing a building owned by someone else. Rental co-ops may share part of the management responsibility and often have more power collectively than single renters leasing from a conventional landlord. Nonprofits can also buy a building and rent it out to lower-income folks who might not be able to afford shares. Sharing a house can offer big savings and can help people avoid foreclosure.

- Market rate co-ops are houses, apartment buildings or other groups of housing units that are organized under a democratically managed corporation in which residents purchase shares at a market rate. Shares cover the costs of a blanket mortgage, rainy day reserves, maintenance and other operating costs, insurance, tax, etc. Units are resold at market rate.

- Limited- or zero-equity affordable housing co-ops receive grants and government subsidies to make co-op shares more affordable to low-income people. They keep the housing permanently affordable through legal restrictions on the amount of gain on a future sale of the co-op share. Often these are organized groups of low-income tenants who agree to collectively buy the building they already rent through a nonprofit, usually a land trust that holds title to the land and takes it off the speculative market. It's a great way to make permanent gains in the fight against gentrification.

A successful limited-equity model is Columbus United Co-operative, a 21-unit apartment building in San Francisco. The San Francisco Community Land Trust (SFCLT)[32] worked closely with the low-income, Chinese-American family tenants who were fighting eviction and demolition. With public subsidy, tenants purchased their units as part of a co-op for little more than their controlled rent in an area where home ownership is half the national average due to cost.

In Los Angeles, Comunidad Cambria went from a gang war zone and drug supermarket slum to a model of peaceful, affordable cooperative housing with the help of co-op housing activist Allan Heskin and several Latina women in the complex. The community rallied to protect its new co-op against threats from gangs and drug dealers to burn the building down, remediated a toxic dump in its basement and created a vibrant community center.

Sunwise Co-op is a rental cooperative, owned by Solar Community Housing Association, with a mission to provide eco-friendly, low-income housing in Davis, CA. The co-op uses solar water heating, photovoltaic panels, passive solar design and composting to reduce its ecological footprint. The members also grow their own veggies for shared vegetarian/vegan dinners and raise chickens and bees. Monthly shares or rental costs at affordable housing co-ops are often half or less of the market cost.

Co-op housing rentals are a relatively easy first step to implement. Co-op ownership can sometimes be a long, difficult process, but with substantial and long-term benefits. If you are thinking about starting your own housing cooperative, here is a basic plan for co-op ownership, much of which applies to rentals as well:

- Find a potentially willing community of people who want to live together long term. Some community cohesion and individual social skills are very helpful. If there isn't already a community, holding dinners or other regular bonding events can lay a good foundation.
- Find a mentor through another successful co-op, a nonprofit that helps develop housing co-ops (such as a local land trust[33] or the California Center for Cooperative Development[34]) and/or a co-op-friendly lawyer. Read the Cooperative Housing Toolkit.[35]
- Educate community members about the entire process. Do an assessment to see if your community has the motivation, finances and skills needed to follow through. (If they don't, you may want to recruit or train people who can help, especially with accounting, legal, organizing and maintenance tasks.) Make a decision whether to move forward.
- Work with a nonprofit or form an independent housing corporation. Form a board of directors from the residents' community with membership, finance,

maintenance and operations/management committees. Create bylaws for organizational procedure, including new-member selection, orientations, decision-making, board and committee elections, regular communication/meetings and conflict-resolution processes. You can use another co-op's bylaws as a model.

- Develop a realistic budget with reserves, then research financing options. If your community is low income, it may be eligible for foundation grants, public subsidies from HUD[36] or municipal affordable housing programs, and loans from Community Development Financial Institutions.[37] Try working with banks that have already funded co-ops; it will be a much easier pitch and process.
- Select the dwelling that you want to buy, convert or construct, and make sure the seller is willing to sell to a co-op.
- Secure a loan and buy the building with the community through a blanket mortgage. This is much easier to secure when working with a nonprofit that has a track record of successful co-op development.
- Complete any rehabilitation or upgrades that are needed in advance of moving in. This can be a fun way to build group cohesion in advance of all living under the same roof.
- Find ways to build community feeling through shared common space, childcare, dinners, group projects or other regular events. Develop relationships with the surrounding community through volunteer programs.
- Although problems can come up, as in any housing situation, the issue most likely to destroy the co-op is internal conflict. Finding the right people and teaching others who are willing to learn how to get along is key.

For more info on how to share housing and other stuff as part of a cooperative, see *The Sharing Solution,*[38] by Janelle Orsi and Emily Doskow, and visit the National Association of Housing Cooperatives website.[39]

SOCIETY

Bad Education
MALCOLM HARRIS

The Project on Student Debt estimates that the average college senior in 2009 graduated with $24,000 in outstanding loans. In August 2010, student loans surpassed credit cards as the nation's single largest source of debt, edging ever closer to $1 trillion. Yet for all the moralizing about American consumer debt by both political parties, no one dares call higher education a bad investment. The nearly axiomatic good of a university degree in American society has allowed a higher education bubble to expand to the point of bursting.

Since 1978, the price of tuition at US colleges has increased by more than 900 percent, 650 percentage points above inflation. To put that number in perspective, housing prices, the bubble that nearly burst the US economy, then the global one, increased only 50 points above the Consumer Price Index during those years. But while college applicants' faith in the value of higher education has only increased, that of employers has declined. According to Richard Rothstein at the Economic Policy Institute, wages for college-educated workers outside of the inflated finance industry have stagnated or diminished. Unemployment has hit recent graduates especially hard, nearly doubling in the post-2007 recession. The result is that the most indebted generation in history is without the dependable jobs it needs to escape debt.

What kind of incentives motivate lenders to continue awarding six-figure sums to teenagers facing both the worst youth unemployment rate in decades and an increasingly competitive global workforce?

During the expansion of the housing bubble, lenders felt protected because they could repackage risky loans as mortgage-backed securities, which sold briskly to a pious market that believed housing prices could only increase. By combining slices of regionally diverse loans and theoretically spreading the risk of default, lenders were able to convince independent rating agencies that the resulting financial products were safe bets. They weren't. But since this wouldn't be America if you couldn't monetize your children's futures, the education sector still has its equivalent: the Student Loan Asset-Backed Security, or, as they're known in the industry, SLABS.

SLABS were invented by then-semi-public Sallie Mae in the early '90s, and their trading grew as part of the larger asset-backed security wave that peaked in 2007. The value of SLABS traded on the market grew from $200,000 in 1991 to $240 billion by the fourth quarter of 2010. But while trading in securities backed by credit cards, auto loans and home equity is down 50 percent or more across the board, SLABS have not suffered the same sort of drop. SLABS are still considered safe investments—the kind financial advisers market to pension funds and the elderly.

In addition to the knowledge that they can move SLABS off their balance sheets quickly, lenders have had another reason not to worry about the loans: federal guarantees. Under the recently ended Federal Family Education Loan Program (FFELP), the US Treasury backed private loans to college students. This meant that even if the secondary market collapsed and there were an anomalous wave of defaults, a lender bailout was built into the law. If that wasn't enough, in May 2008 President Bush signed the Ensuring Continued Access to Student Loans Act, which authorized the Department of Education to purchase FFELP loans outright if secondary demand dipped. In 2010, as a cost offset attached to health reform legislation, President Obama ended the FFELP, but not before it had grown to a $60-billion-a-year operation.

Even with the Treasury no longer acting as cosigner on private loans, the flow of SLABS won't end anytime soon. The loans and costs are caught in the kind of dangerous loop that occurs when lending becomes both profitable and seemingly risk free: high and increasing college costs mean students need to take out more loans; more loans mean more securities that lenders can package and sell; and more selling means lenders can offer more loans with the capital they raise, which means colleges can continue to raise costs. The result is more than $800 billion in outstanding student debt, at least 30 percent of it securitized and the federal government directly or indirectly on the hook for almost all of it.

If this sounds familiar, it probably should, and the parallels with the pre-crisis housing market don't end there. The most predatory and cynical subprime lending has its analogue in for-profit colleges. Inequalities in US primary and secondary education previously meant that a large slice of the working class never got a chance to take on the large debts associated with four-year degree programs. For-profits like the University of Phoenix and Kaplan University are the market's answer to this opportunity.

While the debt numbers for four-year programs look risky, for-profit two-year schools have apocalyptic figures: 96 percent of their students take on debt, and within 15 years 40 percent are in default. A Government Accountability Office sting operation in which agents posed as applicants found that all 15 institutions that were approached engaged in deceptive practices and 4 in straight-up fraud. For-profits were found to have paid their admissions officers on commission, falsely claimed accreditation, underrepresented costs and encouraged applicants to lie on federal financial aid forms. Far from the bargain they portray themselves to be on daytime television, for-profit degree programs were found to be more expensive than the nonprofit alternatives nearly every time.

Despite the attention that the for-profit sector has attracted, including congressional hearings, it's hard to see where the bad apples stop and the barrel begins. For-profits have quickly tied themselves to traditional powers in education, politics and media. Besides being a University of California regent, Richard C. Blum (husband of California Senator Dianne Feinstein), is also, through his investment firm, the majority stakeholder in two of the country's largest for-profit colleges. The Washington Post Company owns Kaplan Higher Education, forcing the company's flagship paper to print a steady stream of embarrassing parenthetical disclosures in articles on the subject of for-profits. Industry leader, the University of Phoenix, has even developed an extensive partnership with *Good* magazine, sponsoring an education editor. Thanks to these connections, billions more in advertising, and nearly $9 million in combined lobbying and campaign contributions in 2010 alone, for-profits have become the fastest-growing sector in American higher education.

If the comparative model is valid, then the lessons of the housing crash nag: what happens when the kids can't pay? The federal government tracks only students who default within the first two years of repayment, but its numbers show the default rate increasing every year since 2005. Only 40 percent of the total outstanding debt is in active repayment, according to analyst accounts, and the majority is in either deferment or default. The Department of Education has begun calculating default rates based on numbers three years after the beginning of repayment rather than two. The results are staggering: Recorded defaults for the class of 2008 have nearly doubled, from 7 to 13.8 percent. With fewer and fewer students earning the income necessary to pay back loans, a massive default looks closer to inevitable.

The government's response to a national wave of defaults that could pop the higher-ed bubble is already written into law—a precaution that was absent in the housing crisis. In the event of foreclosure on a government-backed loan, the holder submits a request to a state guaranty agency, which then submits a claim to the feds.

The advantage of a preemptive bailout is that it can make itself unnecessary: If investors know they're insulated from risk, there's less reason for them to get skittish if the securities dip, and a much lower chance of a speculative collapse. The worst-case scenario seems to involve the federal government paying for students to go to college, and aside from the enrichment of the parasitic private lenders and speculators, this might not look too bad if you believe in big government, free education or even Keynesian fiscal stimulus. But until now, we have examined only one side of the exchange. When a student agrees to take out a loan, the fairness of the deal is premised on the value for the student of the borrowed dollars. If an 18-year-old takes out $200,000 in loans, he or she had better be not only getting the full value, but investing it well, too.

Higher education seems an unlikely site for a speculative bubble. While housing prices are based on what competing buyers are willing to pay, the price of postsecondary education is supposedly linked to its costs (with the exception of the for-profits). But the rapid growth in tuition is mystifying in value terms; no one could argue convincingly that the quality of instruction or the market value of a degree has increased tenfold in the past four decades.

So why would universities raise tuition so high so quickly? "Because they can" answers this question for home sellers out to get the biggest return on their investments, or for-profits out to grab as much Pell Grant money as possible, but it seems an awfully cynical answer when it comes to nonprofit education.

First, where the money hasn't gone: instruction. As Marc Bousquet, a leading researcher into the changing structures of higher education, wrote in *How the University Works* (2008),

> If you're enrolled in four college classes right now, you have a pretty good chance that one of the four will be taught by someone who has earned a doctorate and whose teaching, scholarship, and service to the profession has undergone the intensive peer scrutiny associated with the tenure system. In your other three classes, however, you are likely to be taught by someone who has started a degree but not finished it; was hired by a manager, not professional peers; may never publish in the field she is teaching; got into the pool of persons being considered for the job because she was willing to work for wages around the official poverty line…and does not plan to be working at your institution three years from now.

This is not an improvement. Less than 40 years ago, when the explosive growth in tuition began, these proportions were reversed. Highly represented among the new precarious teachers are graduate students; with so much available debt, universities can force graduate student workers to scrape by on sub-minimum wage, making them a great source of cheap instructional labor. Fewer tenure-track jobs mean that recent PhDs, overwhelmed with debt, have no choice but to accept insecure adjunct positions with wages kept down by the new crop of graduate student workers. Rather than producing a better-trained, more professional teaching corps, increased tuition and debt have enabled the opposite.

If overfed teachers aren't the causes or beneficiaries of increased tuition, then perhaps it's worth looking up the food chain. As faculty jobs have become increasingly contingent and precarious, administration has become anything but. Formerly, administrators were more or less teachers with added responsibilities; nowadays, they function more like standard corporate managers—and they're paid like them too. Once a few entrepreneurial schools made this switch, market pressures compelled the rest to follow the high-revenue model, which leads directly to high salaries for in-demand administrators. Even at non profit schools, top-level administrators and financial managers pull down six- and seven-figure salaries, more on par with their industry counterparts than with their fellow faculty members. And while the proportion of tenure-track teaching faculty has dwindled, the number of managers has skyrocketed in both relative and absolute terms. If current trends continue, by 2014 there will be more administrators than instructors at American four-year nonprofit colleges, the Department of Education estimates.

When you hire corporate managers, you get managed like a corporation, and the race for tuition dollars and grants from government and private partnerships has become the driving objective of the contemporary university administration. The goal, for large state universities and elite private colleges alike, has ceased to be building well-educated citizens; now they hardly even bother to prepare students to assume their places among the ruling class. Instead we have, in Bousquet's words, "the entrepreneurial urges, vanity, and hobbyhorses of administrators: Digitize the curriculum! Build the best pool/golf course/stadium in the state! Bring more souls to God! Win the all-conference championship!"

These expensive projects are all part of another cycle: corporate universities must be competitive in recruiting students who may become rich alumni, so they have to spend on attractive extras, which means they need more revenue, so they need more students paying higher tuition. For-profits aren't the only ones consumed with selling product. If a humanities program can't demonstrate its economic utility to its institution and to students, then it faces cuts, the neoliberal management technique par excellence. Students apparently have received the message loud and clear, as business has quickly become the nation's most popular major.

When President Obama spoke in his 2011 State of the Union speech of the need to send more Americans to college, it was in the context of economic competition with China, phrased as if we ought to produce graduates like we produce steel. As the near-ubiquitous unpaid internship for credit replaces class time, the bourgeois trade school supplants the academy. Parents worried about their children make sure they never forget about the importance of an attractive résumé. It was easier for students to believe a college education was priceless when it wasn't bought and sold from every angle.

If tuition has increased astronomically and the portion of money spent on instruction and student services has fallen, if the (at very least comparative) market value of a degree has dipped and if most students can no longer afford to enjoy college as a period of intellectual adventure, then at least one more thing is clear: higher education, for-profit or not, has increasingly become a scam.

We know the consequences of default for lenders, investors and their backers at the Treasury, but what of the defaulters? Home owners who found themselves with negative equity could always walk away. Students aren't as lucky:

Graduates can't ditch their degrees, even if they borrowed more money than their accredited labor power can command on the market. Americans overwhelmed with normal consumer debt have the option of bankruptcy. But students don't have that choice either. Before 2005, students could use bankruptcy to escape education loans that weren't provided directly by the federal government, but the facetiously named Bankruptcy Abuse Prevention and Consumer Protection Act made all education loans, even credit cards used to pay school bills, non-dischargeable.

Today, student debt is an exceptionally punishing kind to have. Not only is it inescapable through bankruptcy but student loans have no expiration date and collectors can garnishee wages, Social Security payments and even unemployment benefits. When a borrower defaults and the guaranty agency collects from the federal government, the agency gets a cut of whatever it's able to recover from then on (even though it has already been compensated for the losses), giving agencies a financial incentive to dog former students to the grave.

Colleges have benefited from a public discourse that depicts higher education as an unmitigated social good. Since the baby boomers gave birth, the college degree has seemed a panacea for social ills, a metaphor for a special kind of deserved success. We still tell fairy tales about escapes from the ghetto to the classroom or the short path from graduation to lifelong satisfaction, not to mention the US's collective college success story, the GI Bill. But these narratives are not inspiring true-life models; they're advertising copy, and they come complete with loan forms.

Learning Outside the Academy

ERIC MELTZER

Too many people think you need permission to learn something or that difficult things have to be learned in school. However, the prevalence of this attitude is much lower among entrepreneurs than practically any other group. Although going to school to learn things seems to have worked quite well for some of my friends, it's never really been my first choice, so hopefully by explaining alternative strategies for learning I can help out other people for whom schooling isn't an option.

In August of 2008, I decided that I wanted to do my undergrad degree at Peking University (PKU) in Beijing, instead of applying to schools in the States. I had spent an incredible summer in Beijing as an intern in a lab at Peking U, and I was determined to get in. My idea was that I'd spend the five months before the admissions deadline in an immersion program and pick up enough Chinese to pass the admissions tests. As it turned out, there are no immersion programs except the Defense Language Institute (only open to military members, oops) that will teach you Mandarin in that span of time. I decided I'd learn it on my own, and here are some notes (cleaned up a bit) that I wrote after I was admitted to PKU and managed to pass all of my first-semester classes. I've since found that these lessons are applicable to more than just studying languages:

1. Make a curriculum. Breaking a big concept like "fluency in Mandarin" (or "learning to program in Lisp" or whatever) into concrete pieces is step one. Often what you choose to skip is as important as what you learn. I asked my mentors and friends exactly what I would need to make it through my first year at Peking University, and the consensus was that I could skip learning how to write characters and how to read classical Chinese, in order to focus hard on speaking, listening and reading. I've ended up going back to the things I skipped, but the order was really important, and trying to do it all at once would have been disastrous.

2. Make practice as close to the real thing as possible. Instead of using materials intended for students, I played a game where I'd enter all the characters I encountered in daily life into my phone, and they'd all get dumped into a flash-card program at the end of the day. This meant that every character I learned was a character I had run into on the street, with absolutely no time wasted on esoteric or outdated stuff taught in classes. To practice listening, I watched movies and paused at lines I didn't understand. To practice speaking, I talked at every opportunity (and there were many.) As a side note, the effect that the attitude of native speakers toward foreign learners of a language has on one's ability to learn quickly can't possibly be overstated. For this reason I think Mandarin Chinese is easier to learn than French or Japanese; in Beijing, coming off as unfriendly or aloof is considered extremely rude, which is not the case to the same extent in either Tokyo or Paris.

3. Genius doesn't have much to do with it. Schools and parents in the US emphasize intelligence over effort in a bunch of subtle ways, whereas in Asia, effort and dili-

gence are the focus. Regardless of what side of that debate you come down on, if you've decided to learn something, deliberating about your own natural talent for that thing does absolutely nothing for you. Tanaka Ikko, one of the founders of Muji and a graphic designer of extreme skill, told a student complaining about his own lack of natural design sense, "First is strength. Second is strength. There is no third or fourth. Fifth is sense." This isn't machismo, it's just a better understanding of how mastery is actually acquired.

4. Find something you can pour yourself into happily. Don't bother trying to learn anything you aren't truly interested in. When I was learning Mandarin I didn't think twice about spending hours in front of a flash-card program drilling characters; this sounds strange, but it really wasn't unpleasant at all. Each character brought up many associations, and the thrill of being able to read a little bit more of the newspaper each week kept me going. Obviously there will be difficult periods, but if you find yourself miserably plodding forward for any significant period of time, quit and go learn something you actually enjoy.

5. Find teachers. Not going to school for something does not mean you should go without teachers. Accomplished mentors are usually delighted to take motivated students. Finding a really good teacher for something will let you learn way faster than you could otherwise, and no matter what they charge per hour it'll be cheaper than paying tuition at a school. Good teachers are actually really undervalued monetarily, especially in the United States (not so much in places like Hong Kong, where top tutors make seven figures), so spend as much as you can on good instruction whenever you find it. Skillshare is a

great way to find solid teachers, and you'll benefit also from meeting lots of other people studying what you're studying.[40]

Quite a few other tactics are useful for people learning outside of the academy, such as book selection, peer groups and the discipline of time management. The trick is to keep looking until you find what works for you.

Occupy
Everything
WILLIE OSTERWEIL

Spain: The Indignant Community

Towering over the people-occupied Placa Catalunya, in Barcelona, Spain, a five-story tall Hyundai ad reads, "Una altra forma de penser és possible" ("A different kind of thinking is possible").
But Hyundai didn't really believe it themselves.

It's 2 a.m. on Monday, June 20, 2011, and
1,000 Indignados are still in the plaza, dancing, drinking and
watching YouTube videos of yesterday's protests in Athens,
Madrid, Lyon and elsewhere that are showing on the camp's
projector screen. It is a well-earned celebration. The Spanish
media is reporting a turnout of between 100,000 and 150,000,
but the Pirate Commission (Placa Catalunya's resident hackers)
have crunched the photographs and are reporting that 275,000
people took to the streets of Barcelona today. To put that into
perspective, Barcelona's greater metro area has a total population of three million. At the height of the march, around 6 p.m.,
protesters filled the streets all the way from Placa Catalunya, the
march's starting point, to Pla de Palau, its end; a wall of protes-
tors two miles long. Around the globe, early estimates predict
that five million people took to the streets in solidarity.

After two weeks of rain, conflict, delay and media blow-
back, this is a major victory for the Barcelona *Indignados*.
They have led a global day of protest larger than any seen
since the 2003 lead up to the Iraq war. There are weeks,
months, even years of hard work and struggle ahead, but

tonight the men roaming the square selling one-euro beers and samosas are doing brisk business. Cigarette smoke hovers in the air; the leaders behind the commission desks are smiling for once; and couples sneak off to the tents for a little privacy.

What makes this even more incredible is that planning for today's actions began only two weeks ago. The protests were coordinated to coincide with the EU vote on Euro management for the upcoming year. I have to repeat myself here: five million people were mobilized world wide in two weeks.

The 15 May movement caught almost everyone by surprise. The Spanish millennials had been dismissed as apolitical and apathetic, certainly incapable of starting a movement of mass revolutionary consciousness. But change was coming. In the early days of the fiscal crisis, Spain's Creative Commons community politicized, expanding their mission away from the Internet and toward social change. Abortive youth protests in 2009 and intensive online political discussion had many of those involved in the Spanish free culture movement expecting something to happen. But no one expected this.

It's been a little over a month since the Facebook-organized protest on May 15 that defied all expectations and led to the founding of the camps, but everything has organized with incredible speed. It began with 40,000 more or less strangers refusing to leave Placa Catalunya. On May 17, "Commissions" were formed to solve individual problems within the camp. For the next couple of days, these were basically groups of six or seven people, sitting a semi-circles in the middle of the square or under improvised bivouacs, talking. Now, a month later, there are 18 commissions, all with their own tents and booths. And not just the clearly necessary action, communication and infrastructure commissions; there are also commissions of agriculture, health and even theater. At first, the entire camp held a general assembly once a day. Now, commission representatives hold public meetings three times a week to discuss the progress made by their groups and plan actions for the camp moving forward.

On May 15, protesters slept on the ground, if they slept at all. By May 20, camping tents, toilets and tarp covers for a couple of commissions had been erected. Today, there is a kids' playroom filled with donated toys, a people's library, a free store for clothing, and a massage and meditation tent. The camp has power (electricians hacked into the grid, and there are donated back-up generators), Internet (the Pirate Commission has built and provided private servers), even printers, scanners and all variety of audio visual equipment (provided by the A/V Commission, naturally). When I arrived two weeks ago, the plaza was covered in beer and wine stains, and garbage littered the square. Now, they sweep and mop three times a day, and campers walk around picking up garbage regularly.

The camp feels magical, but it's also totally jerry-rigged, improvisation built upon improvisation: tape, string, tarp, cloth, metal tent poles holding up a sagging canvas roof, plastic sheets propped upon three long bamboo rods taped together. A truly massive storm could take the whole thing down—but can't the same be said of the status quo? This camp, if joined by enough like it around the world, could be that storm.

June 19 was a massive success: the protests were completely peaceful and were so large that the US media actually took notice (even if they claimed *Los Indignados* want "economic reform" rather than revolution). A movement that is built so fast feels precarious; the fact that it appeared so quickly makes its sudden disappearance seem equally plausible.

I have no idea whether the *Indignados* will succeed, or, if so, what kind of a world they will build. They are learning and organizing at an incredible rate, and though they do not share an ideological worldview (beyond a total dismissal of political parties, politicians, bankers and police), they have a functioning praxis of all-inclusive participatory democracy. Ideology, decisions and actions are built every day from the ground up.

Most of the people here in Placa Catalunya are hungry; all of them are exhausted; and they're smoking way too many cigarettes. But they are happy, creative, inspired, committed and, most importantly of all, living free lives. It sure seems like they're not leaving camp any time soon. Who would want to?

The Park And The Protests

It's Tuesday, September 27, 2 p.m., and another general assembly is beginning here in Zuccotti Park, a small park at the corner of Broadway and Liberty in Manhattan's financial district, two blocks from the World Trade Center site, three blocks from Wall Street. Zuccotti, renamed "Liberty Plaza" by its occupiers, has been held as a home base by protesters for ten days. This, in itself, is a kind of achievement. In the general assemblies leading up to the September 17 day of protest that culminated in the occupation, organizers hoped that the occupation would last days, weeks, perhaps even months, but no one could guarantee it would make it six hours. Yet hundreds are here, on day ten, holding another open discussion of tactics, infrastructure and politics. Even five days ago this wasn't a foregone conclusion.

Rain during the week resulted in dwindling numbers, though there were never fewer than 100 people in the square, and media coverage was either dismissive or outright malicious.[41] Police pressed with random arrests and threats of eviction. Still, numbers surged over the weekend, and people gathered for a huge street-taking march on Saturday. Saturday's march, with numbers somewhere between 700 and 1,000, was met with dramatic police brutality[42] and mass arrests,[43] the largest mass arrests in New York City since the protests at the Republican National Convention in 2004. Videos of police throwing protesters to the ground and pepper spraying women from close range spread widely across the Internet and have led to an explosion in numbers here and a shift in the tenor of news coverage.[44]

Inspired by the methods of the Arab Spring and the protest movements in Israel, Greece and Spain, protesters from New York City and the rest of the country (I spoke with one man who had come from Alaska) have built an encampment of sorts; so far, tents and structures have been taken down by the police, so people have slept out in sleeping bags. Police presence and instruction has, thus far, been a major problem: Zuccotti is surrounded by cops without and crawling with them within: blue shirts and lieutenants walk freely through the square, and protesters foolishly follow the rules set out by the police. I've watched plainclothes officers enter the square, pump protesters for information and then walk straight back out to talk to their superiors. TARU, the New York Police Department's (NYPD) intelligence unit, has been constantly on the scene, and I can only guess at the number (tens?) of undercovers. NYPD is using Occupy Wall Street as an intelligence-gathering bonanza, and if, as I believe, Zuccotti is the beginning of a serious movement here in NYC, we're giving the cops everything they need to know: who is friends with who and who has sway and organizational ability. That is a serious tactical problem that protesters have yet to address. Still, numbers are growing every day and are buoyed by appearances in the general assembly of Michael Moore, Cornel West, Susan Sarandon, Lupe Fiasco and Immortal Technique.

As the general assembly grows, major meetings with everyone in the square become unwieldy and incredibly difficult. There is a need to shift decision-making to smaller groups, and it would be great to see a focus on neighborhood organization: general assemblies in the boroughs would be an incredible achievement. As with the movements in Spain and Greece, occupiers have eschewed simple demands or sound-bite messaging. As elsewhere, there is no official representative body that speaks for the protesters, no centralized or formally hierarchical power structures. The lack of a clear, easily regurgitated message tends to enrage both the media and the traditional and professional left, but the demandless occupation is not a reflection of stupidity, political impotence or idealistic naïveté, as many within and without the protests have claimed. Such claims only reveal the impotence and poor analysis of their makers.

On February 15, 2003, the largest protest in the history of humankind was organized and carried out. Between 10 million and 30 million people participated globally, with about 500,000 protesters in New York City alone, all around an incredibly simple demand: don't go to war in Iraq. Thirty-three days later, "combat operations" began. The demand couldn't have been clearer. Eight years on, dozens of Iraqis die in bombings every day.

And what about Vietnam? Ten years of escalating protest, and the movement shattered itself, exhausted, against an implacable imperial war machine. The unifying demand—the end to the Vietnam War—gave meaning and direction to the protests and helped build the solidarity of the student movement, but when the demand itself was met, and the Vietnam War ended, the movement splintered into a thousand pieces. And it was not some innocent failure of well-intentioned people: in the anti-war movement's collapse, the black community was betrayed and abandoned by the majority of their white "comrades." Their leaders murdered or jailed, the radical black movement was abandoned by a white middle-class left fleeing the fight like American diplomats helicoptering out of Saigon. Many of these hippies, radicals and student protesters of the Vietnam era went on to become the very parents, bosses, landlords and teachers who have helped destroy this planet with abject consumption, raise the price of universities only to make a degree worthless, "globalize" financial capital so that wage slavery and precarity reaches every corner of the globe, etc. These same ex-hippies make up much of the professional left and media commentatoriat who tell us we need one clear demand.

When we look around us, we see a world that is burning, a planet being consumed by capital, an economic system that thrives on the production of human suffering, mass imprisonment, violence, economic strife. We see a world that cannot be fixed by the same people who brought us here, with the same methods, ideologies and processes. And we see that we are not going to win the fight tomorrow. But we want to win. We're going to win. So we do what we can. We take a space, we build our resolve and our numbers. With every day that we hold the square, we chip away at our fear, at our confusion, at our alienation. We improvise new ways of living, new relations, new forms of solidarity. We create. We meet each other. We share food, sleeping space, music and drink. We fight the cops together. We talk about what a new and better world would look like, and we try, to the best of our abilities, to build it.

And, as we discuss our ideas and principles in Liberty Plaza, it becomes clear that, though we may have different focuses, different politics, though different goals brought us all here, we can achieve them only by working together. We are preparing ourselves for the fight ahead because we have been left futureless by a group of people who insist we ask them to solve the problem, so they can refuse us. We don't make one simple demand because this isn't for the media to turn into sound bites, for politicians to aggrandize or argue against, for bankers to gamble on and academics to study. We're not asking the people in power for permission, we're teaching ourselves how to take what we need and make a better world without them.

The Battle of Brooklyn Bridge

"Whose Bridge?"

"Our Bridge!"

"Whose Bridge?"

"Our Bridge!"

For one hour on that Saturday, the Brooklyn Bridge belonged to the people. One thousand protesters spilled over its roadway while another thousand marched across the pedestrian walkway. In the roadbed, filling the Brooklyn-bound lane with traffic, we screamed and jumped and took in the view. And not the view from the narrow, raised central walkway, where there isn't nearly enough room for the tourists and bikers to coexist, where ten-foot high metal construction barriers have recently blocked the skyline. We were right up against the edge.

For the next four hours on Saturday, the bridge belonged to the NYPD. Setting a line of police vehicles and orange netting at the center of the bridge, and coming up behind us with patrol vans and paddy wagons, they kettled us (a police maneuver for managing large crowds by corralling them into a cordoned area). Some protesters, quick enough and closer to the center, scaled the bridge posts onto the safety of the walkway ten feet above, but cops soon pushed through the northeast side of the lane, separating us from escape. One by one, violently at first, then, as the reality of our position became clear, smoothly, they arrested us. The NYPD spent four hours arresting 700-plus people.

We were put in plastic cuffs and set down behind the police barricades, where an "arresting officer" was assigned to every five protesters. From then on we would be transported and processed in groups of five, getting in and out of jail at the same time, a little sub-unit of solidarity. Some of us were put in police vans and buses, but most were transported, like I was, in requisitioned city buses. Ours was a B41, which normally runs right by my apartment, driven by a regular bus driver—a coerced union transportation worker, not a cop—who said while we rolled out, "It feels like the '60s again!" to raucous applause. Aching arms restrained behind us, seated on the hard plastic seats, cops standing over us looking bored, with our eyes at their waists, looking at their guns and pepper spray, this was the commute par excellence.

There is no single precinct jail with capacity for 700 prisoners, so protesters were spread in jails across Manhattan and Brooklyn. The buses functioned as holding cells while the police prepared intake—mobile arrest pens where we sat for hours needing to pee and stretch our arms and legs. For most of us that was the worst of it. Arresting officers didn't get to leave until their five arrestees were processed, so we sat in jail talking, chanting, singing, sleeping or staring sullenly at our feet while they filled out paperwork until two, three, four in the morning. Those of us with ID and without warrants were given a bench summons for disorderly conduct and released the same night; those without ID were released throughout the day Sunday. Though a couple of protesters with outstanding warrants stayed longer, many protesters with, shall we say, pressing legal issues got through unscathed. We overwhelmed them: the cops just didn't have the capacity to properly sort us. Charges would've been disastrous, but there were too many arrestees, and as a result, barely any misdemeanor charges (let alone felonies) were laid.

But for all that happened, the stories parsing the meaning of Saturday's events have focused around one ten-minute stretch: the moment at which people deviated from the pre-planned route across the pedestrian walk and took the roadway. Two stories are being told. Story one claims that the police instigated and tricked protesters onto the road, luring them with a combination of obviously weak policing and agent provocateurs in order to entrap and arrest them. The idea that cops led protesters onto the bridge has largely been supported by a video that shows police walking ahead of protesters as they enter the on-ramp, which has been interpreted as cops leading the march.[45]

Story two has the protesters stopping their march at the base of the on-ramp to make a choice. The police warn them to get out of the road, but a group of protesters in the front decide to link arms and take the bridge anyway. The lieutenants, not expecting this radical action, back off, and protesters march onto the bridge with cops fleeing ahead of them. This argument has been supported by a video in which a lieutenant, announcing protesters' imminent arrest if they don't clear the road, is ignored and drowned out by marchers' cries.[46]

In story one, the NYPD are brilliant tacticians, controlling and understanding the protesters perfectly. Despite this total knowledge, however, they are so filled with spite for the protesters that they are willing to shut down the Brooklyn Bridge for five hours to arrest them, resulting media coverage be damned. They're supposedly both super-villain brilliant and obsessively idiotic. In story two, the police are

SHARE or DIE

unprepared and overwhelmed. Expecting the protesters to cross legally, the majority of the police force was amassed on the Brooklyn side. When protesters took the bridge, the Brass panicked and locked down the bridge. They arrested everyone, believing it better than appearing unable to control the situation, revealing themselves as reactive, arrogant and tactically mediocre.

In the first story, the protesters are foolish, misled and chaotic, unable to recognize that they're being led by the police to certain arrest. Idealistic but stupid, fatally infiltrated by provocateurs, they bumble away from the planned peaceful march into disaster. Despite their total idiocy, this narrative maintains, these innocents are the very center of the police's universe, the total focus of their actions. In story two, the protesters recognize their own strength, the power-and-attention-amplifying value of disrupting infrastructure and the potential fun of occupying the bridge. They overcome their fear of the police and their fear of the impossible, and they seize their own freedom, even if just for an hour.

The protesters should clearly be telling story two, and not just because it's what actually happened. But instead, they've mostly told the former. Why? The generous explanation is a knee-jerk dismissal of mainstream media and police narratives, which is certainly present, but there are worse motives for the propagation of the cop-control story: vanguardist plots, power grabs or preemptive surrender. Despite all disavowal, power has centralized around certain figures within Occupy Wall Street's committees, and when power centralizes, its bureaucrats always try to hold onto it. So organizers blame the other side, albeit with a blatantly bizarre explanation. (The cops really wanted to shut down the Brooklyn Bridge and arrest 700 people? Their whole job is to keep infrastructure functioning.) Organizers, upset over the loss of control of the march and behaving identically to police upset over loss of control of the bridge, blame the other side. Each side argues that its own weakness took the day.

Those of us running up the Brooklyn Bridge, those of us who for one glorious hour held it, occupied it with 1,000 of our closest friends, weren't manipulated by police: we just decided we'd take a walk on the bridge. Everyone focuses on the arrests, on the drama, but most people fail to mention just how easy it is to take over something when there are 700 of you. One thousand people can walk anywhere they want, and, if they do it right, do anything they please. It's when the cops are trying and failing to arrest 1,000 of us that things are going to get really interesting.

10 Ways Our World is Becoming More Shareable

We're sharing more things, more deeply, with more people. Why sharing is the answer to some of today's biggest problems.

NEAL GORENFLO & JEREMY ADAM SMITH

Sharing is a big deal these days. Sharing is a growth industry, a new field of study and of practice; it presents a realm of career opportunities, a new way of life, and a concept around which we are restructuring our world. Sharing is the answer to some of today's biggest questions: How will we meet the needs of the world's enormous population? How do we reduce our impact on the planet and cope with the destruction already inflicted? How can we each be healthy, enjoy life, and create thriving communities?

— Janelle Orsi,[47] co-author of *The Sharing Solution*

Our world is inherently shareable, though it's easy to take that for granted. We are historically connected by climate, roads, oceans, language, forests, culture and social networks, all of which are shared as commons.[48] But in recent decades, the rules of access and ownership have started to shift in new directions, making sharing more convenient, necessary, fulfilling and even profitable. Here are 10 ways that our world is becoming more shareable.

1. Sharing as a Lifestyle. The ways to share in everyday life seem to be multiplying like rabbits, but maybe the Great Recession is forcing all of us to pay more attention these days. Carsharing, ridesharing, bikesharing, coworking, cohousing, tool libraries, and cooperatives are all on the rise.[49] And ways to share power, dialogue and knowledge, such as workplace democracy, citizens' deliberative councils, unconferences and world café are getting more attention these days.

There are also scores of new websites—like Airbnb.com (peer accommodations), Thredup.com (kid clothes), Chegg .com (textbook rental), Neighborgoods.net (general sharing), RelayRides.com (peer-to-peer car sharing), Hyperloca vore.ning.com (garden sharing), Zimride.com (ridesharing), Skillshare.com, Vayable.com (experience sharing) and more—designed to help us share. Taking all of these into account, it's entirely possible to create a complete lifestyle based on sharing. You can live in a cohousing community, work in a co-op, grow food in your neighbor's yard, and get to the open space town council meeting via your car share. A shift in emphasis from ownership to access—taking possession of an asset only when we need to use it—can liberate us from the burdens of ownership such as the high costs, maintenance, insurance, taxes, storage and disposal.

2. Shareable Cities. A revolution is underway in our understanding of cities. It couldn't come any sooner, considering that 2007 was the first year in human history that the majority of human beings lived in cities. Perhaps as a result, cities are becoming the focal point for our collective hopes and dreams, as well as all kinds of innovation needed to avert worsening environmental and economic crises.

In the past, we tended to see cities as dirty, unnatural and isolating places; today, citizens and urban planners alike are starting to see their potential for generating widespread well-being at low financial and environmental cost. There's increasing appreciation for the benefits of public transit, urban agriculture,[50] making room on the streets for pedestrians and bicyclists, and for civic engagement.[51] The very thing that defines a city—its population density—makes sharing easier, from cars to bikes to homes.

Perhaps in response, there seems to be a boomlet in technology that helps First World urbanites understand their environment, share, and use urban resources more efficiently. IBM based their massive Smarter Cities advertising campaign around this theme. But it may be that the most successful innovations will spring from the megacities of the developing world. In the absence of vast financial resources, these cities may do as Bogotá, Colombia[52] did and prioritize human well being over economic growth through investing in commons such as schools, parks, and public transportation.[53] Can a city become a happiness commons? Former Bogotá mayor Enrique Penalosa knows from experience that it's possible.

3. Social Enterprise & Cooperatives. Definitions vary, but in general social enterprises, whether nonprofit or for-profit, offer a product or service in order to advance a social or environmental mission with benefits for all. The industry is small relative to the overall economy, but growing extremely fast in some sectors:

- Over 11,000 worker cooperatives have emerged in just the last 30 years, many them embracing prosocial missions in addition to being managed, governed, and owned by the people who work at them.[54] Whatever the type of coop, over 800 million people in the world belong to these member-controlled economic networks, and they employ more people than multinational corporations.[55]

- Fair trade good sales doubled between 2004 and 2007 to around $4 billion[56] and grew by 24% in 2010 alone.[57]
- Social investing could grow to $500 billion in assets under management in 5–10 years, according to the Monitor Institute.[58]
- Nonprofit earned income grew over 200 percent to $251 billion between 1982 and 2002.[59]

4. The Nonprofit Sector. Nonprofits are an increasingly important way for people to share their wealth and labor, especially as the recession grinds on. With community engagement and social enterpreneurship an increasingly important part of everyday life, Bill Drayton may be right: We may yet evolve into a world where everyone is a change-maker.[60]

- About 75 percent of all donations in the US come from private individuals like you and me.
- In 2010, the US volunteer rate was 26.3 percent, with 62.8 million volunteers donating approximately 8.1 billion hours of service worth an estimated $173 billion.[61]
- In the US alone, donations to nonprofits more than doubled between 1987 and 2007, to $303 billion.
- Nonprofits employ around 10% of the workforce in the US.

5. Microfinance is a powerful innovation that extends small loans and financial services to help the world's poorest rise out of poverty, serving customers traditional banks ignore. The growth of Nobel Peace Prize winner Muhammad Yunus' Grameen Bank, and its success in alleviating poverty in Bangladesh, helped trigger an almost unmanageable surge of money into the sector. There was an estimated $38 billion in outstanding loans and 78 million borrowers at the end of 2009.[62] Grameen has low-interest loan programs for a variety of poor borrowers, including no-interest loans, and is owned by the rural poor it serves. Kiva, a US nonprofit peer-to-peer microfinance sensation, facilitates around $8 million in no-interest loans a month to entrepreneurs in developing nations through its website.[63] At one point, Kiva had to limit loans through their platform because the demand to give out loans was so high. Microfinance is yet another way the world is learning to share its wealth.

6. The Internet. It's easy to take it for granted, but its potential as a platform for sharing has arguably just begun to unfold. The Internet itself would not be possible if people did not share labor, code, and infrastructure. No one owns it or runs it. It's built and it operates on free and open source software and open standards. Data travels over networks and is routed through servers owned by private individuals and corporations who share transport and routing duties.

This global commons enables the creation of tremendous value. Harvard Business School professor John Quelch estimates that the economic impact of the Internet is $1.4 trillion annually in the US alone.[64] This year, the Computer and Communications Industry Association calculated that companies and nonprofits relying on "fair use"[65] (such as search engines, web hosts, and social media) employ 17 million people and generate $4.7 trillion a year, one sixth of our Gross Domestic Product.

All of that value is created on top of what is essentially volunteer sharing on a massive scale. As late as 1992, IBM did not think such a network was possible. Through its runaway success, the Internet has become the model for organizing life in the twenty-first century, as well as the essential infrastructure and distribution channel for commerce, ideas, work, and play. And its influence reaches far beyond the online world. The Internet is reprogramming culture to the degree that society will likely be remade in its image, so that we have a better chance at thriving like it does.

7. Free and Open Source Software (FOSS). FOSS and the Internet have a symbiotic relationship. The Internet would not have been possible without FOSS. And the growth of FOSS relies on the Internet to power its peer production and distribution model. Over 270 million people use the Firefox browser, a shared, freely available tool. Half of the world's Web sites, about 112 million, run on Apache Server, also open source. A quarter of a million websites run on Drupal, a leading open source content management system.

That's just scratching the surface: Today, there are over 200,000 open source projects with nearly 5 billion lines of code that would cost an estimated $387 billion to re-produce.[66] Check out the Infoworld's Open Source Hall of Fame[67] for more on desktop favorites, like Ubuntu, as well as obscure but vital infrastructure projects like BIND. You might also check out the Open Source Census,[68] which tracks business installations of FOSS.

Today, millions of people and organizations rely on FOSS for their daily work, as do a growing number of governments. It's a pervasive part of life in the developed world—and be-cause of its low cost, open source may become even more important to developing countries.

8. The Open Way. Inspired by the success of free and open source software, the values and practices of open source—opening contribution and access to collective creations to everyone—are being applied in a truly dizzying number of ways. In just the last few years, peer-to-peer sharing and co-production strategies have gained significant traction in science, business management, manufacturing, culture, education, and government. Applications of "the open way" range from the obscure, like the open source tractor,[69] to the everyday, like the OpenStreetMaps project.[70] To get a sense of the scope of the movement, check out the P2P Foundation,[71] Opensource.com, and David Bollier's excellent book on the topic, *Viral Spiral*.

9. Social Media. Sharing is the currency of social media. And as Socialnomics writer Erik Qualman, says, social media is bigger than you think.[72]

- More video is uploaded to YouTube in six months than was produced by the three major TV networks in 60 years.
- If Facebook was a country, it would be the fourth largest country in the world by population with over 800 million users.
- Wikipedia has almost 4 million articles,[73] all written by volunteers—and with an accuracy that studies show is comparable to the best commercial encyclopedias.
- Ninety-six percent of Generation Y has joined a social network, where sharing is a way of life.
- Creative Commons has made it easier for creators to share their work. They've licensed over 400 million creative works in 63 countries since 2002.

In these powerful ways, social media has taken sharing mainstream and paved the way for the use of the Internet to share more real stuff in the real world.

10. Generation G. Now that a Shareable world has a serious foothold, all that's needed is a willing population to scale it up. There's a strong argument that Gen Y is the generation that can bring a shareable world to fruition.

Roughly 100 million strong in the United States alone, Gen Y grew up on the Internet and brings its values and practices, including sharing, into the real world. In 2009, TrendWatching.com called them Generation G (for "generosity") and said they are accelerating a cultural shift where taking is "the new status symbol."[74] They may not reach their full sharing potential until later in life, but there are promising indicators:

- Sixty-one percent of 13–25 year olds feel personally responsible for making a difference in the world.[75]
- Eighty-three percent will trust a company more if it's socially and environmentally responsible.
- The Arab Spring, the UK anti-cuts movement, the 15-M movement in Spain, and the Occupy movement were arguably spearheaded by this generation.

Author and strategist Gary Hamel believes that this massive generational force, which outnumbers baby boomers, promises to transform our world in the image of the Internet, a world where sharing and contributing to the common good are integral to the good life. William Strauss and Neil Howe, authors of *Millennials Rising*, believes that Gen Y is a hero generation, coming of age in a time of crisis they're already helping to resolve, largely by applying the tools and mindset of sharing.

NOTES

1. Robin Marantz Henig. "What Is It About 20-Somethings?" *The New York Times Magazine.* August 18, 2010. http://www.nytimes.com/2010/08/22/magazine/22Adulthood-t.html.
2. shareable.net/users/emigennis.
3. emergentbydesign.com/
4. emergentbydesign.com/future-of-money-project/.
5. emergence.cc/futureofmoney/.
6. bit.ly/e3xVyG.
7. bit.ly/gO22NA.
8. kck.st/flBNzH.
9. www.swiftcommunity.net/communities/225/detail.
10. 1.usa.gov/bpapuo.
11. For a humorous look at the effectiveness of a bachelor's degree, visit bit.ly/hEqhqa.
12. A video by *The Atlantic* explores the issue of home ownership versus rental: bit.ly/zg2sxq.
13. For an explanation of collaborative consumption, view the speech by Rachel Botsman at a TED event in Sydney, Australia in 2010: bit.ly/AsLnQu.
14. See scr.bi/aHRAgA.
15. See Neal Gorenflo's article "Is Social Media Catalyzing an Offline Sharing Economy?" at bit.ly/fI59dr.
16. For ideas on ways to share, visitshareable.net/how-to-share.
17. collaborativeconsumption.com/.
18. For information on this, visit bit.ly/gauEYp.
19. See bit.ly/hkJYs0.
20. See bit.ly/Aow7dm.
21. See bit.ly/1Lp9RT.
22. Rachel Botsman. *What's Mine Is Yours*. HarperBusiness, 2010

23. For information on this organization, visit iamyoung detroit.com/.

24. on.fb.me/AsiFQS.

25. Doxie's blog about her homeless project is at littleds world.blogspot.com/.

26. georgiastreetcc.com/.

27. You can learn more about the initiative at bit.ly/ypciMW.

28. flickr.com/photos/johnthac/.

29. bewelcome.org/.

30. couchsurfing.org/.

31. casarobino.org/.

32. sfclt.org/.

33. cltnetwork.org/.

34. cccd.coop/.

35. cccd.coop/files/HousingToolbox.pdf.

36. portal.hud.gov/hudportal/HUD.

37. cdfi.org/index.php

38. Janelle Orsi and Emily Doskow. *The Sharing Solution: How to Save Money, Simplify Your Life & Build Community.* NOLO, 2009.

39. coophousing.org/.

40. skillshare.com/.

41. For an example of media coverages, visit nyti.ms/xVISPN.

42. bit.ly/ohGKod.

43. nyti.ms/yURLsN.

44. For an example of media coverage, visit on.msnbc.com /oE9VC6.

45. bit.ly/q381Aq.

46. bit.ly/zf6GAx.

47. Janelle Orsi. "Four Degrees of Sharing." shareable.net/ blog/four-degrees-of-sharing.

48. bit.ly/aeI77k.

49. Car sharing: bit.ly/GURZ7a; Taxi sharing: bit.ly/GULMtM; Bike sharing: bit.ly/GUS6j5; Coworking: shareable.net/ blog/the-state-of-coworking; Cohousing: bit.ly/GW0q0s; Tool libraries: shareable.net/blog/four-degrees-of-shar-ing; Cooperatives: bit.ly/9uUw0W

50. bit.ly/1KlNbr.

51. bit.ly/dimK5g.
52. bit.ly/eRJrLN.
53. bit.ly/53HNwK.
54. Maria Armoudian. "The Economic Revolution Is Already Happening: A Q&A with Gar Alperovitz." bit.ly/GUMCGU.
55. shareable.net/blog/2012-international-year-of-the-co-op
56. Fair Trade Federation. "Facts and Figures." bit.ly/q1OB1x
57. *The Independent.* "Fairtrade market experiencing explosive growth in UK and US." ind.pn/fw7FAM.
58. Monitor Institute. "Executive Summary." *Investing for Social and Environmental Impact*, p. 12. bit.ly/3XOuGo.
59. Tony Ramsden. "Ask an Expert: Tony Ramsden on Earned Income." bit.ly/GUbVYH.
60. Bill Drayton. "Everyone a Changemaker: Social Entrepreneurship's Ultimate Goal." bit.ly/GWf5f5.
61. VolunteeringInAmerica. "Volunteering in the U.S." volunteeringinamerica.gov/national.
62. Wikipedia. "Microfinance." bit.ly/9UMZ8u.
63. kiva.org.
64. John Quelch. "Quantifying the Economic Impact of the Internet." hbswk.hbs.edu/item/6268.html.
65. wired.com/wired/archive/13.08/tech.html?pg=4.
66. Stephen J. Vaughan-Nichols. "How Many Billions Is Open Source Software Worth?" bit.ly/Tbrsx.
67. bit.ly/GUMLKs.
68. osscensus.org.
69. blog.opensourceecology.org/2008/09/progress.
70. openstreetmap.org.
71. openstreetmap.org.
72. Erik Qualman. "Statistics Show Social Media Is Bigger Than You Think." Socialnomics. bit.ly/b6Dy7
73. bit.ly/12E3xv.
74. "Generation G: The Would Be G for 'Generosity,' Not G for 'Greed.'" trendwatching.com/trends/generationg.
75. Sharon Jayson. "Generation Y Gets Involved." *USA Today*. usat.ly/OJupK.

ABOUT THE AUTHORS

Malcolm Harris is a writer based in Brooklyn, focused on education and generational politics. He's a contributing editor to Shareable.net and an editor of The New Inquiry.

NEAL GORENFLO is the co-founder and publisher of Shareable.net, the leading online magazine about the sharing lifestyle and economy. He's a former Fortune 500 strategist turned social entrepreneur. In addition to his work at Shareable, he's a board director of ForestEthics, a forest protection nonprofit, and of Independent Arts & Media, a nonprofit committed to civic expression and dialog.

SHAREABLE.NET, the original source of Share or Die's stories, is a nonprofit online magazine that tells the story of sharing. Shareable covers the people and projects bringing a shareable world to life. And shares how-tos so you can make a sharing real in your life.

In a shareable world, things like car sharing, clothing swaps, childcare coops, potlucks, and cohousing make life more fun, green, and affordable. When we share, not only is a better life possible, but so is a better world.

Go to Shareable.net for sharing news, tools, and tips plus the largest collection of sharing how-tos on the web.

If you have enjoyed *Share or Die,*
you might also enjoy other

BOOKS TO BUILD A NEW SOCIETY

Our books provide positive solutions for people who want to
make a difference. We specialize in:

Sustainable Living • Green Building • Peak Oil
Renewable Energy • Environment & Economy
Natural Building & Appropriate Technology
Progressive Leadership • Resistance and Community
Educational & Parenting Resources

New Society Publishers

ENVIRONMENTAL BENEFITS STATEMENT

New Society Publishers has chosen to produce this book on recycled paper
made with **100% post consumer waste,** processed chlorine free, and old
growth free.

For every 5,000 books printed, New Society saves the following resources:[1]

20	Trees
1,835	Pounds of Solid Waste
2,019	Gallons of Water
2,634	Kilowatt Hours of Electricity
3,336	Pounds of Greenhouse Gases
14	Pounds of HAPs, VOCs, and AOX Combined
5	Cubic Yards of Landfill Space

[1]Environmental benefits are calculated based on research done by the Environmental Defense
Fund and other members of the Paper Task Force who study the environmental impacts of the
paper industry.

For a full list of NSP's titles, call 1-800-567-6772 *or visit our website* at:

www.newsociety.com

new society
PUBLISHERS